NO ONE TOLD ME!

An Honest Look at Ministry

James E. Hightower, Jr.
EDITOR

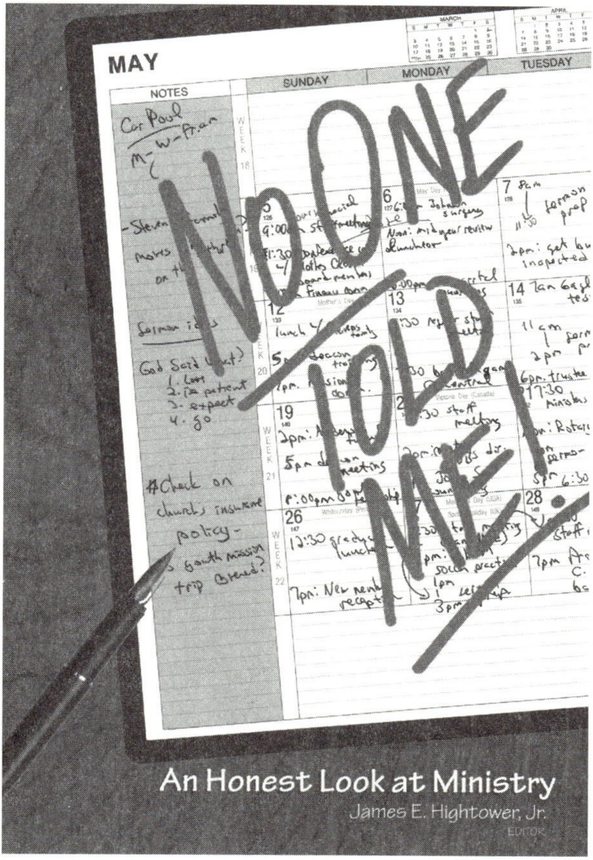

Chronicles of Narnia
C.S. Lewis

Contributors

Larry Baker, pastor, First Baptist Church, Pineville, Louisiana

Hardy Clemons, pastor, First Baptist Church, Greenville, South Carolina

Jim Hightower, minister of pastoral care, First Baptist Church, Huntsville, Alabama

Dave Long, pastor, First Baptist Church, Bermuda

Ann Melton, free-lance consultant and writer; former minister to singles, First Baptist Church, Huntsville, Alabama

Martin Thielen, pastor, Grace United Methodist Church, Mt. Juliet, Tennessee

Scott Walker, pastor, First Baptist Church, Waco, Texas

No One Told Me!
An Honest Look at Ministry

Editor
James E. Hightower, Jr.

SMYTH & HELWYS
PUBLISHING, INC.

Macon, Georgia

ISBN 1-57312-153-3

No One Told Me!
An Honest Look at Ministry

James E. Hightower, Jr.
Editor

Copyright © 1997
Smyth & Helwys Publishing, Inc.
6316 Peake Road
Macon, Georgia 31210-3960
1-800-747-3016

All rights reserved.
Printed in the United States of America.

The paper used in this publication meets the minimum
requirements of American National Standard for Information
Sciences—Permanence of Paper for Printed Library Materials.
ANSI Z39.48–1984

Library of Congress Cataloging-in-Publication

No one told me!: an honest look at ministry/
    editor, James E. Hightower, Jr.
    viii + 88 pp.   5.5" x 8.5" (14 x 21.5 cm.)
    Includes bibliographical references.
    ISBN 1-57312-153-3   (alk. paper)
    1. Church management.
    2. Clergy—office.
    3. Church work.
    I. Hightower, James E.
    BV652.N6   1997
    253—dc21   96-37770
                                                               CIP

Contents

Editor's Note vii

You Can't Get Your Blessing from a Church 1
    Why are you driven to please your church members?
    Can the church give you a sense of self-worth?
    How do you make peace with your past?

Whose Vision Is It Anyway? 11
    Just what is vision, anyway?
    Is vision a theory or an action?
    How can you lead a congregation to
    overcome past problems and develop vision?

Sunday's Coming—Again 31
    Have you noticed that Sunday comes
    every seven days whether you are ready for it or not?
    What is an appropriate form of worship?
    How can you order worship so that it is biblically
    grounded and sensitive to the needs of the congregation?

Be Prepared: Fights Are Inevitable 47
    Can peace exist in the local church?
    Is conflict always bad?
    How do you deal with church problems?
    Can you survive church fights?

Lone Ranger or the Brady Bunch: Working as a Team 57
    How can you experience
    a sense of community with other ministers?
    How do you lead the staff and congregation toward teamwork?
    What is the role of the team leader?
    How can differences between staff members be handled?

Finding and Nurturing Volunteers: The Never-Ending Task 71
    How do you staff the many jobs in a church?
    Is there really someone to fill every volunteer position?
    How much freedom *or* supervision is appropriate for volunteers?

No One Told Me!

No One Told Me I'd Be Supervising People 79
Can you demand quality work from volunteers?
Can you fire volunteers?
How can you inspire volunteers to dedication and hard work?

Editor's Note

This is a book born out of our love for local churches and our gratitude for the theological educations we received. We all give thanks for the churches we have served, especially the churches we currently serve.

We also give thanks for those who taught us during our theological studies. Especially are we grateful for those individual professors who helped us on our way:

—Larry Baker, for William L. Hendricks
—Hardy Clemons, for Boyd W. Hunt
—Jim Hightower, for D. Elton Trueblood
—Dave Long, for Frank Stagg
—Ann Melton, for Philip H. Briggs
—Martin Thielen, for E. Glenn Hinson
—Scott Walker, for Bryant Hicks

I am especially grateful to First Baptist Church, Huntsville, Alabama, for a study leave during which time I completed this book. To the pastor and people of First Baptist Church, Bermuda, who welcomed the Hightower family into their pasonage and me into their pulpit, I give great thanks. To my friend, Dan Martin, who encouraged me to redream this project when my first effort failed, I say thank you for believing in the worth of this book. I am deeply indebted to my wife, Cathy, for believing in my ministry, teaching me to use my computer, correcting my grammar, and choosing to be my companion.

I have attempted to leave each contributor's style intact. The joy of working with this group of people is that each is a highly competent professional minister who has given their heart to Jesus Christ and their mind and hands to Christ's church. The people I have shared this project with are also some of my closest friends. To them I say thanks for friendship and for sharing with me the ministry of writing.

No One Told Me!

To you the reader, some ministers serving local churches already, some seminarians preparing to serve local churches, this book is offered with the hope of more effective ministry.

Jim Hightower
The Baptist Parsonage
Devonshire, Bermuda
July 31, 1995

You Can't Get Your Blessing from a Church

Scott Walker

I received an excellent seminary education. Attending the Southern Baptist Theological Seminary during the early 1970s, the school was at the height of its prowess and strength, its faculty ranks filled with world-renowned scholars. I fondly remember Dr. George Beasley-Murray who opened the New Testament world to me and gave me a lifelong love for biblical exegesis. Dr. Glen Hinson intrigued me with his stimulating lectures on church history, and Dr. Wayne Oates served as both guide and mentor as we walked down the very personal and introspective passages of pastoral care. These were rich years, the greatest intellectual challenge of my life.

Upon graduation, however, I was not aware that my education as a minister was only beginning. I was soon to discover that many things would confront me as a professional minister for which seminary did not—and perhaps, could not—prepare me. One of those things was coming to terms with my own sense of inadequacy and my insatiable need to please others. I soon learned that successfully dealing with this one primal issue can make or break a minister.

The Problem

What am I talking about? I am convinced that many, if not most, professional ministers have an inordinate need to please their church members or constituencies. Now, a certain amount of the desire to please and be popular is normal and healthy. Our longing to be loved and accepted by significant others is vital to emotional and spiritual health. But some very gifted and skilled ministers literally turn their lives into twisted pretzels by trying to please and mollify everyone. The tragic result is professional burnout, depression, and disillusionment.

No One Told Me!

A typical example is a scenario that happens to every pastor sooner or later. It is noon on a Sunday morning, and you are standing at the door of the church. The choir is singing the final measures of the benediction response. You are weak-kneed, and wiping sweat from your brow. For the last twenty-five minutes you have poured your heart and soul into a carefully crafted sermon. Now, it is a vulnerable time. Already you are itching to ask your spouse the weekly question: "How did I do, Honey? What did you think of my sermon?"

Your parishioners file by, and you quietly tally the vote. Mrs. Williams' voice sounds the prevailing opinion, "I really liked your sermon today. It spoke to me." Without moving your lips or losing professional dignity, a grin stretches from ear to ear. It is wonderful to be loved and appreciated.

Then, at the end of the line, looms dour Mr. Brown. With the weight of the world on his shoulders and piety oozing from every pore, he intones, "I love you, brother, but we do not agree. When you have lived longer, you'll see things differently." Off he walks into a glorious afternoon, having dumped his rain on your parade.

On the way home, you fume. Dozens of people expressed in verbal and nonverbal ways their love and support for your thoughts, your ministry, and your personhood. But this one man—the church sourpuss—has robbed you of your good mood, your afternoon nap, your romp with the kids, your sense of self-worth. His lonely voice thunders above all others. He has made your life miserable.

Yet, at a deeper level, you sense that the real problem is deep within you. Why have you given this one man so much power? Why has he been able to stifle the dozens of voices of those who affirm and support you? Why are you upset that you have not pleased this one man? Why are you so hypersensitive to the opinions of other people? And why must you satisfy everybody? These questions gnaw at you. They point to an important and unresolved issue in your life, a dynamic popularly called "the blessing."

The Blessing

What is the blessing? This term comes from our Jewish heritage. The Hebrew root word we translate as "blessing" literally means "to speak well of" or "to praise." The opposite of "to bless" is "to curse."

In the strongly paternalistic milieu of the Old Testament world, there was an important familial rite of passage called the blessing. In this rite, it was the duty of the father to give his sons—particularly the eldest—his blessing. Often, this blessing was given near the time of the father's death as an act of bestowing inheritance. This form of the blessing is poignantly pictured in the book of Genesis, when blind and ailing Isaac called his oldest son Esau to kneel before him so that he might place his hands ceremoniously upon his head and give his son the blessing. But Jacob, the younger son, tricked his father and older brother. He knelt before the blind old man, disguised as Esau, and Isaac unwittingly gave Jacob the paternal blessing (Gen 27:1-40).

The blessing meant far more, however, than just receiving inheritance and possessions. It also spoke of the father's love, acceptance, and praise of the son. It signified that the father "spoke well" of his child. Symbolically it said to the young man, "You are pleasing to me. You are worthy of my trust, my lineage, my love, the profit of my lifetime. I am proud of you."

Most significantly, the blessing—though accumulated over the course of years—could be officially given only once, and the action was irrevocable. The blessing could come to a boy only from his father and was for all time. Whether or not a Hebrew son received his father's blessing had a tremendous impact on his future. Esau grieved forever that Jacob had stolen his father's blessing. As an ancient Jewish maxim states, "The blessing of the father builds the children's house."[1]

Today the term "the blessing" is used to describe a very important emotional and psychological dynamic that transpires between parents and their children.[2] This dynamic centers around whether or not children grow up feeling that their parents—both father and mother—"speak well of them" or "praise them" and, in short, give them their blessing. Though this sense of blessing is not given in an official ceremony, as in ancient times, it is nonetheless meted out verbally and nonverbally throughout childhood and adolescence. By the time teenagers leave home to face their own uncertain future, they intuitively know whether or not they have received the blessing, or even a partial blessing.

When children are fortunate enough to enter adulthood after having, over the years, received the cumulative blessing of their parents, then they are prepared to "build their house" in the world. But without the parental blessing, a sense of self-doubt and a lack of self-worth can be so prevalent that the basic building blocks for constructing a life of happiness and self-fulfillment are simply not available. This means that the presence of the parental blessing upon one's life is a major factor in the mental and emotional health of adults.

The Withheld Blessing

Why would the parental blessing ever be withheld from a child? Certainly, to ask such a question conjures up thoughts of parents who do not love their children, who are coldhearted, selfish, and irresponsible. And yet many people who struggle with a lack of blessing come from homes where their parents truly loved them and where much hard work and concern were directed toward providing for their basic needs. Why, then, is a sense of blessing often not adequately developed or communicated?

We must begin answering this question by making a crucial qualifying statement. It is a fact that few children ever grow into adulthood feeling they have fully received the parental blessing. At best, a child knows that the major aspects of his or her life are pleasing, accepted, and affirmed. And yet there are some remaining areas where the blessing is missing. Receiving the blessing is usually not an either/or proposition—we have it or we don't. More often it is a matter of degree. Most of us will leave home positioned between the diverse polarities of feeling "mostly blessed and accepted and enjoyed by my parents" to the more painful feeling of being "mostly rejected, misunderstood, and a disappointment to my parents." Somewhere between these two extremes our niche is carved by the wear and tear of years of family interaction. Most of us cannot be fully blessed. That is an unrealistic expectation. We can have the hope, though, that we will be mostly blessed.

Driven to Be Blessed

What happens if deep within us—often at a subconscious level—we do not feel that we have been adequately blessed? Usually we become driven by an insatiable need to get somebody else to give us their blessing. This somebody else can be a coach, a teacher, a spouse, an employer, and—in the case of ministers—our church members. Faced with an aching void of lack of self-worth, we are constantly in search for somebody else to fill our emptiness with words of affirmation, praise, and support. Yet, the tragedy is that we are walking down a dead-end street. We cannot get somebody else to give us the parental blessing.

I have experienced this dynamic in my own life. I have wonderful parents and come from a very healthy family. But I missed the blessing in at least one important aspect of my life.

My grandfather was a Colorado rancher and a true pioneer. He built a successful ranch out of sparse barren land and lived by the sweat of his brow. He pushed his three sons and two daughters to labor hard, and the greatest compliment you can receive in our family tradition is to hear the words, "You are a good worker!"

A generation later, when I was a young teenager living in the Philippine Islands where my parents were missionaries, I began to go through some typical adolescent rebellion. Far more interested in sports and girls than in work and academics, I let my grades drop, my hair grow long, and I took a pretty "laid back" attitude toward life. One night, my "slide toward decadence" came to a climax with my cowboy father.

I had brought home a very mediocre report card. My father, a seminary professor, was incensed. When he tried to talk with me about the matter, I acted disrespectful. He exploded. Taking me by the arm and leading me outside on the porch for a little nose-to-nose confrontation, he gritted his teeth and said, "Scott, your laziness is going to be your downfall. God has given you a good brain, and you are simply not using it. Now, if you can't learn to be a good student and work hard, I'm going to send you home to the ranch and, by God, you can sure learn how to sweat and use your hands. I'm tired of your goofing off!"

With these words, he wheeled around and walked back inside, leaving me fuming and shaken by the experience. Unfortunately, Dad died of a heart attack several months later and walked out of my life as well. We never had time to resolve our conflict. A part of the blessing was never bestowed. And I never forgot a message spoken in haste and frustration: "You are lazy . . . and a lousy student!"

Fifteen years later, I was the pastor of my first church and full of vim and vigor. I was putting in long sixty- and seventy-hour weeks. I wanted to do my job right. My sermons were carefully researched, manuscripted, and published each week for the congregation—evidence of good scholarship. And I was perpetual motion—visiting the sick, reorganizing the office, working with the youth, meeting with every committee—and proud of my long hours of work.

One day, the chairman of the deacons took me to lunch. In the midst of conversation, this wise and older man looked me in the eye and said, "Scott, you've got to slow down. You can't keep up your hectic pace. We want you to be with us a long time. You'll burn out if this pattern keeps up."

His words were music to my ears. I respected his opinion very much. Rather than hear and heed his warning, I felt he was giving me the blessing I hungered for. He was bestowing the family motto upon me: "You are a good worker." I basked in the glow of the moment.

Rather than take his advice, however, I worked harder. And sure enough, a year later I was exhausted, feeling depressed, and wondering what was wrong with me. Clearly I had become a driven person, driven by a lack of blessing in my life. And nobody—the deacon chairman, the personnel committee, my wife—could give me the blessing I had not received from my father. I still felt compelled to prove that I was a conscientious student and a "good worker."

The Catch-22

Again, we must look to one of the central tenets of the Old Testament blessing. *Only the father could bestow the blessing upon the child.* And from our understanding of psychology, we know that only the *mother and father* can bestow the parental blessing upon their children. When this blessing is partial or nonexistent, a person can go through life insatiably demanding from others a blessing they cannot give. Such demands and expectations, when not openly recognized, can destroy friendships, marriages, and professional relationships. For to demand the blessing from those who cannot give it is to insure a constant feeling of frustration, disappointment, and resentment within significant relationships.

Now, to the point. Many ministers are men and women who have not adequately received the blessing. Their lack of blessing has often, in a convoluted way, turned them into "caregivers." Like a middle child who is lost between the blessed older child and the pampered and adored younger child, it is discovered that the easiest way to seek the blessing is to be "the good boy/girl," "the peacemaker," the "loyal servant," or the "dedicated and friendly pastor." And like the lost middle child, you will do back flips in hopes of finally squeezing a blessing out of somebody.

Again, the only problem—the Catch-22—is that when the primal parental blessing of childhood is missing, all of the compliments and affirmation from friends, mentors, and parishioners will not fit the bill. Like an overweight person who has had a surgical stomach bypass, you can swallow all of the food (affirmation) you want, but it cannot bring nutrition to your starving soul.

Making Peace with Your Blessing

So what do you do? This is an age-old question, and it is not easy to answer. My response may frustrate you, but I must be honest.

In an earlier book, *The Freedom Factor*,[3] I discussed several things people can do to help them come to peace with a lack of blessing. Though they are good and healthy suggestions, to list them here might short circuit and derail you from doing the one primary thing that is essential to healing. That one thing is to make an appointment with a competent pastoral counselor and spend some hours telling your story and discussing your feelings about your blessing.

Coming to grips with your blessing is not something you can do by reading a self-help book or reviewing the events of your life in the safety of solitude. It just will not work. Rather, it requires walking down the pathway of your past with a good and trusted friend. To put it another way, you are going to need a pastor yourself to work through your struggle with the blessing. And you cannot really be an effective pastor or counselor until you have allowed someone to be a pastor to you. As the wise Swiss physician and therapist, Paul Tournier, once wrote, "We can become fully conscious only of what we are able to express to someone else."[4]

There are no shortcuts or easy answers. If you have recognized your own struggle in the mirror of this short chapter, then perhaps you need to be good to yourself, make an appointment with a pastoral counselor, and heal that struggling little child way down deep inside of you.

We were taught a lot of wonderful and essential things in seminary. But few of us were taught how to take care of ourselves in a professional world that can eat you alive. Most of us will struggle with lack of blessing along the way. That is to be human. But we do not need to struggle alone. And we do not need to struggle without the hope and assurance of God's healing.

Notes

¹Jesus Sirach 3:11, Gerhard Kittel, ed., *Theological Dictionary of the New Testament,* vol. 2 (Grand Rapids: Eerdmans, 1964) 754ff.

²Though the psychological term "the blessing" is frequently used in theological circles and can be attributed to no specific person, I am indebted to Dr. Myron C. Madden for his writing and popularization of this concept. Particularly helpful are his books *The Power to Bless* (Nashville: Abingdon, 1970), *Claim Your Heritage* (Philadelphia: Westminster, 1984), and *Blessing: Giving the Gift of Power* (Nashville: Broadman, 1988).

³R. Scott Walker, *The Freedom Factor* (San Francisco: Harper & Row, 1989).

⁴Paul Tournier, *The Meaning of Persons* (New York: Harper & Row, 1971) 17.

Whose Vision Is It Anyway?

Larry Baker

> Despite my ideological disagreements with my father, I have always respected the fact that he had a vision for America. Though I've quarreled with the implementation of that vision, without some kind of vision for a country or a relationship, there is little hope.[1]

So writes the author of *Angels Don't Die,* in which Patti Davis reflects on the lessons she learned from Ronald Reagan that she has never forgotten. Reagan's daughter capsuled the president's vision—"a shining city on the hill, a strong, prosperous nation"—and depicted the shaping power of that dream in his political career.

Others in our time have lived by some vision. Two of the best known were Martin Luther King, Jr., and John F. Kennedy. During the early 1960s as I launched my ministry, their words and voices captured my emotions and imagination.

Nevertheless, when I finished seminary for my first place of full-time ministry, I usually associated vision with prophets such as Ezekiel and seers such as John on Patmos. I had listened to preachers, mostly evangelists, sermonize on the King James translation of Proverbs 29:18, "Where there is no vision, the people will perish." but, I had not so much as heard of George Barna or other bestselling gurus of vision; nor had I considered the importance of vision in the work of the minister.

What I did have was first-class preparation for ministry. Some of my teachers had challenged me with images and concepts related, I now know, to vision. T. B. Maston did, with his rubber band image of the minister's task of keeping tension on the people of God. C. W. Scudder did, with his focus on the Old Testament prophets' use of "ought" and their dream of God's kingdom established in the human order. William Hendricks did, too, as he marched us through biblical, historical, and contemporary theologies and urged us to translate those into the tongues of ranchers in the cedar-strewn, limestone hills of central Texas, and executives in pine-shrouded, azalea-laden northeast Louisiana. We did not, however, deal with vision in the 1990s meaning of the word.

Adding "Vision" to the Lexicon

Vision is the 1990s watchword in the ministerial manual. During the years since my time as a fledgling minster, we have focused on a double handful of ministries and ministry issues. We have pursued nontraditional and noncongregational forms of ministry and contemporary worship of several kinds. We have plunged into social action and social ministry and pursued pastoral counseling and twelve-step therapies. We have developed skills in conflict management and ministry management. We have worked at small groups, the marketing of the church, and countless styles of preaching. We have concerned ourselves with spiritual formation, the case method, and church growth. We have pursued church renewal and lay leadership. But we have dealt with vision only recently.

George Barna faults seminaries for failure to deal with vision. He charges that "most Protestant seminaries in this country virtually ignore vision as a critical dimension of ministry." He argues that "the evidence is quite convincing that our seminaries fail to treat vision with the respect and emphasis accorded to it even by our most average, secular graduate schools of business."[2] Barna also blames Christian intellectuals, theologians, teachers, and authors who apparently refuse to address the subject of vision. He contends that "few Christian authors have addressed the topic directly" and have failed "to take the discussion to a deeper and more practical level."[3] Perhaps, perhaps not.

One fact is clear: Vision is new to other professionals as well. According to James Kounzes and Barry Posner,

> Until recently, vision was not part of the management lexicon. We might have heard it uttered by human potential psychologists, but it did not pass over the lips of business people and management scholars.[4]

Whose Vision Is It Anyway?

Today that has changed. Scholarly work on leadership is now brimming with treatments of vision. Likewise, popular magazines tell the stories of "visionaries" and picture the power of vision in corporate culture and common life alike.

In this final half-decade of the twentieth century, I, like many other ministers, have been thinking much about vision. I have been thinking about the meaning of the concept and its sources, the process of developing and communicating it, the parameters and the impact of vision. I have also implemented some of my discoveries and have discovered some of the payoffs.

Warren Bennis,[5] Stephen Covey,[6] Max DePree,[7] and the American Management Association[8]—not George Barna—put me to thinking about vision. Bennis grabbed my attention while I served as Vice President for Academic Affairs and Dean of the Faculty at Midwestern Seminary. The work of Covey and DePree and the publications of the Association have shaped my viewpoint and actions since coming to First Baptist Church, Pineville, Louisiana, in mid-1988.

Eyes Fixed on a Better Country

"Just what is vision, anyway?" I first asked as I listened to and read Warren Bennis. Isn't it a new way of packaging and reserving leadership and administrative ideas like leftovers from last night's dinner? Not so, if you take people such as Robert Belasco[9] seriously.

Vision is essential to successful leadership in corporate America and congregational life alike, but it resists easy definition. According to Calvin Miller, "Vision is the photographic image that guides a pilgrimage to the goal it depicts."[10] Barna thinks it is "the big picture, a comprehensive sense of where you are, where you are going, and how you're going to get there."[11] Karl Albrecht, however, likens vision to "the northbound train" that sets the direction and powers the engine of an organization as it moves on a clear track toward the future.[12] Bob Dale pulls an image from nature and tells us that vision is "a potent steering current [that] directs our work."[13] According to Bennis and Nanus, vision is "a mental image of a possible and desirable future state of the organization."[14] "At its simplest level," according to Peter Senge, "vision is the answer to the question, 'What do we want to create?'"[15]

As I distilled the discussions of the meaning of vision, I identified four characteristics. (1) Visions are future-oriented. Visions are statements of destination, of the ends of our work. (2) Visions are our windows on the world of tomorrow. Through vision, we get a picture of what things will be like before we have begun the journey. Visions are images in the mind. (3) Visions express one's sense of the possible. Vision expresses possibilities and potential; it speaks of "what can happen positively" and "what can be." (4) Visions are unique and set apart from everyone else. They tell persons inside and outside alike what is different about one's church.

Vision paints a picture of where visionaries want the church to go and what they want it to be. However, vision doesn't require that every policy, strategy, and specific program be worked out in detail.

Where There Is No Vision

Everyone who writes or speaks about leadership spotlights the importance of vision. Consider Lyle Schaller. "What is needed?" he asks in *44 Steps off the Plateau.* He answers: "First, someone must have a vision of what God is calling the congregation to be and to do in the years ahead."[16] Hear George Barna: "Realize that true ministry begins with vision. For a Christian leader—that it, an individual chosen by God to move His people forward—vision is not to be regarded as an option."[17] Reflect on Bob Dale's words: "Leaders need a sublime idea, a vision of future possibilities. We need the commanding force in our lives."[18]

As I considered the meaning of vision, I took a new look at Proverbs 29:19, "Where there is no vision the people perish; but he that keepeth the law happy is he." Usually this text is used as the rationale for some grand scheme—a building project, establishment of a new congregation, or the relocation of an existing one. We often read into Proverbs the picture we might have of what we can do to reach our goals and to enlarge our ministry and program instead of the intended message of the writer.

The sage was not thinking in such terms, however. The primary meaning of the text has to do with the prophetic vision. The writer was thinking of the word from God that guides God's people into truth.

Where there is no word from God, the people lose all restraint. Where there is no prophetic vision, "people run loose rather than have vision and goal and focus and structure as to where they are going," observed James Carter.[19] Thus, the New International Version translates that verse, "Where there is no revelation, the people cast off restraint."

Proverbs 28:19 is an antithetical proverb. On one hand is the picture of a people who have no prophetic vision, no guiding words from God, and thus cast off all restraint and run loose without any kind of goal or focus or structure. On the other hand are those who keep and honor the law, the revealed will of God. The second group is happy because there is a focus to what life with God ought to be and life has a goal. When there is vision, God's people hear the guiding word from God that portrays what the church might be.

A Laboratory for Vision

In 1988, First Baptist Church was a laboratory for vision that embodied a sizable challenge. For almost two decades, the church had struggled intensely and declined sharply. One of my predecessors retired after almost twenty-seven years, at a time when the church proudly completed a two-story activity building but rumbled internally with conflict. My two immediate predecessors left for various reasons, but both the victims of forced resignation.

Other internal developments depleted the church's spirit. A youth minister left to pursue seminary studies; a beloved minister of education died following a short bout with cancer; and a minister of music retired from active ministry because of health problems. For a brief period during the early stages of my tenure, I was the only professional minister on the staff.

Contextual factors took their toll on the church's psyche as well. The state experienced severe economic reversal, and the immediate region knew double-digit unemployment. Banks and savings and loan corporations collapsed; businesses folded. An out-migration of population occurred, and the area saw its congressional district swallowed up in redistricting. The England Air Force Base, an economic bulwark in the region for four decades, was shut down by the federal government, its personnel reassigned, and its business and tax revenues lost.

Conflict and circumstances produced heavy casualties. Hundreds of members departed to other churches as the victims of disillusionment or the result of taking sides on controversial matters. Others relocated within and beyond the state. Many who stayed moved to the sidelines of church life. Some who stayed banked the embers of resentment and waited for a place to fan them into flames of confrontation. Others remained with their commitment in place but their spirits bruised and their hearts weary.

Buildings showed the damage, and corporate life pictured the hurts of the two decades preceding. Stained, frayed, and torn carpet covered the floors. Dingy, faded, peeling paint covered the walls of the sanctuary. Educational spaces for preschoolers and children and their parents were neglected, dilapidated, and rundown. Youth met in areas built a quarter century earlier but untouched since.

The church's organizations were also in shambles. Committees remained unstaffed and often inactive. A few people gave themselves willingly to Bible teaching, music, and mission programs, but many led only spasmodically and halfheartedly. Few volunteered for service; others said "yes" with reluctance.

"What's a Nice Church Like You . . . ?"

Almost four years into my pastoral service, I raised a question in a Sunday morning sermon: "What's a nice church like you doing in a place like this?" I noted that this is a timeworn and familiar question. Sometimes it expresses surprise: "Look at this place. I can't believe that someone like you would be found in a place like this!" Sometimes it calls for explanation: "How in the world did you ever end up in a situation like this? How could you get yourself into this?" The question could call for other answers. It could ask, "Why did you decide to do this?" or "What are you involved in? What actions are you taking here?"

"People sometimes ask a similar question of a church," I noted. I recalled a conversation between two pastors. One asked the other why "his church" was located as it was. The building was magnificent, built with red brick and white columns. It was spacious, with ample educational building, roomy sanctuary, and plenty of parking.

But the neighborhood was something else. Across the street was a strip shopping center, a hodgepodge of tiny shops for the most part. Down the street, little more than a block away, were topless bars and nightclubs. In the next block were liquor stores, pawn shops, a cheap hotel, and low-cost housing.

The questioning pastor wondered why a church would choose to build in a location like that. He wondered why a church would choose to stay in a neighborhood like that. "What's a nice church like yours doing in a neighborhood like this?" was his question.

"That is a good question for any church and for every congregation," I said in 1992, and have said often since. It gets at the reason for the church's being, the purpose for the church's life. It also raises questions about the church's life, ministries, and activities. It asks us to think about what we are trying to accomplish through the life of the church.

"Think about our church," I invited. Then I said something like this: "On the second Sunday of January, 1911, a tiny band of people met and organized the Pineville Baptist Church. Thomas Howell tells us that

> On Sunday, January 8, 1911, Rev. E. O. Ware preached at 11:00 A.M. and 7:30 P.M. at a tabernacle at the far end of Reagan Street in Pineville. The service was not unusual: a recollection describes it as "a little singing, a little preaching, and a little talking about organizing." Ware . . . was evidently inspirational, for at the conclusion of the services those present agreed to organize the Pineville Baptist Church.[20]

"That was eighty-one years ago. The church has lived through the Roaring Twenties, two world wars, the cold war, the Korean War, the Vietnam War, and Operation Desert Storm. It has survived the Great Depression and a series of financial recessions. It is older than the Cooperative Program, four of our Southern Baptist seminaries, and at least a half-dozen of our denominational agencies and commissions. The people who started the church in 1911 'came to stay' and 'stay' we have."

"Why did they organize in the first place? Why have they stuck with it for more than eight decades now? What is a nice 'First' church like this one doing in a place like this?" I inquired.

Then I suggested, "We can answer the questions in several ways. We can put our answer in a single sentence: We are here because we are Christ's people doing Christ's work in our world, beginning in this community. Or, we can use three words to answer the question: We are following, bringing, and caring. We are following Christ; we are bringing good news; we are caring for others. Here is our reason for being; here is the shape of our life. Here is what brought us here, and here is what we're up to while we are here."

During that sermon, I asked the question three times: "What's a nice church like yours doing in a place like this?" Each time I responded: "Answer first with the word, 'Follow.'" Then, "Answer now with the word, 'Bringing.'" Again, "Use a third word to answer, 'Caring.'"

Whose Vision Is It Anyway?

As I concluded, I recounted an anecdote from the life of Mother Teresa. I noted, "For thirty years Mother Teresa has worked in the slums of Calcutta, India. She has worked among the most forsaken people on earth. You and I would recoil from most of the people she touches every day—the dispossessed, the downtrodden, the diseased, the desperate. Yet, everyone who meets Mother Teresa comments on her warm smile. How after thirty years of working conditions like that does she keep a warm smile on her face?"

Then I suggested, "Well, that's interesting. She says that at age eighteen she left Yugoslavia to become a Christian servant. She said, 'When I was leaving home, my mother told me something beautiful and very strange. She said, "You go put your hand in Jesus' hand and walk along with him." ' That has been the secret of Mother Teresa's life ever since."

"That's our answer," I said. "That's why the church is here. We have our hands in Jesus' hand, and we are walking with him. We are Christ's people doing Christ's work in our world. Following Christ, bringing good news, caring for others—that is reason enough for us to be here and reason enough for us to give it our best!"

Crafting the Vision

"What's a nice church like you . . . " served as a transition. It was both end and beginning, the wrap-up of a process of vision shaping and the launching of a new look toward the future. I took the first step during my installation service as pastor. I said, "I have not come to be a contemporary David doing battle against the giant of the modern world while you, the host of Israel, stand back in your pews watching to see how he fares. We—you and I—have a common ministry and common mission. So we Bakers have come to minister *with* you as our church family takes hold of Christ's mission and ministry in *this* place."

During the months following, I acted as pastor, coach, cheerleader, trainer, visionary, therapist, facilitator, and advocate.

Sometimes, in one-to-one sessions, I was confrontational; publicly, I was always encouraging and supportive and visionary. I used every occasion possible to talk about our calling and our future.

Then I took the next step. I invited key laypersons to talk with me about our church and its ministry. Men and women from every stage of adulthood and every sector of the church's life came. Several dozen spent a Saturday morning in discussion with me. A couple dozen deacons met with me at dinner one evening. We talked about the church's ministry needs as we formed search committees for staff positions and looked for persons to fill them. We talked about the church's mission during finance committee meetings and as we developed budgets year-by-year.

The culmination of this phase came one evening when several dozen men and women joined me for dinner and discussion at a local restaurant. We talked and prayed about our mission as a church. We discussed three questions:

- Why have a Baptist church in Pineville?
- What should a well-rounded Christian be doing, and how can the church help that happen?
- What is the church's responsibility to those inside the church and to those outside?

Then we heard reports from seven small groups. As they reported, I recorded their responses on newsprint taped to a wall. When we concluded, we had summarized our mission thus:

Following Christ
Bringing Good News
Caring for Others

Next, I wrapped up our plenary session with the suggestion that our responses mean that we will be people and our church will be a place where love comes to life. I did not give the vision; it emerged from the men and women in that room. I was the first to articulate it in the image we adopted. Soon thereafter, I said to the church, "Here is the flag around which we shall gather. Here is the music to which we shall march. Here is the theme for our life together and for our ministry. Here is the goal for all that we do. Here is the standard by which we shall measure. Here is God's vision for us. Together, through God's strength, we can accomplish it. We can, through God's strength, be people and a church where love comes to life."

Watching the Vision Come to Life

My reading recorded countless stories of visionary success. In the world of business, leadership stars such as Steven Jobs and Stephen Wozniak of Apple, Fred Smith of Federal Express, Lee Iacocca of Chrysler, Ray Kroc of McDonalds, and Buck Rodgers of IBM dominated the economic night sky. In the world of church, pastoral leaders such as Bill Hybell stood out as the epitome of vision. Robert Schuller capsuled the stories of a dozen of his disciples who "made their dreams happen." Schuller declared that "by combining great faith with great ideas, these amazing men and women are achieving great things for God." *Leadership* profiled three successful vision stories in its summer 1994 issue. These stories, the reporters suggested, "breathe life into the dry bones of vision. They help vision take on flesh and blood."[21] Schuller expressed the mind of others and himself when he wrote, "As you read their thrilling stories, you will be given a vision of the future for your own church as well."[22]

Throughout my life, "what I did" and "here's what happened" accounts have frequently caught my eye, perhaps because verbatims and case studies were significant parts of my seminary training, and because biographies and autobiographies have been favorite fare since my first trip to the public library at age seven. Thus, I read with interest, as well as with a dose of skepticism, the reports of successful vision. The anecdotes, vignettes, and chronicles encouraged me to think that there "really is something to this vision business." I decided to give it a shot!

No One Told Me!

Now, I am eyewitness to the shaping power of vision. During a seven-year period, First Baptist Church:

- developed a church mission statement with supportive graphic art, public relations, and outreach materials and stationery
- sent youth mission teams to Appalachia, Baltimore, Ann Arbor, North Little Rock, Seattle, Western Colorado, and Rochester
- ordained two female deacons and one female minister, the first in the church
- renovated the sanctuary at a cost of $400,000, debt-free at the time of completion
- adopted, for the first time in its history, a master plan for its buildings and campus
- launched a $2.6 million renovation project in its oldest education spaces
- started a ministry to single adults
- restructured and revitalized the church's daycare and weekday early education program
- developed Advent worship including an annual presentation of a music drama prior to Christmas
- started a full, summer-long children's ministry for grades 1-6 in addition to its traditional Vacation Bible School and employed a summer minister to children
- established an inner city, multiethnic mission
- welcomed more than 700 persons into its membership

Additionally, the church completed several small projects beyond the budget: for example, the purchase of new hymnals, pew Bibles, vehicles, and property.

I watched the shaping influence of a shared vision in other ways. Four groups of laypersons demonstrated it as they went about their work: the committee on committees, nominating committee, deacon nominating committee, and deacon officers.

The work of the deacon officers exemplified the work of all. The diaconate was chaired by the forty-four-year-old executive director of a state mental health agency. The chair, two officers, and four committee chairs served as the deacon leadership team. Responsibility for motivating and guiding the diaconate rested upon them.

These six came to their roles when the diaconate was largely dispirited and functioning poorly. For several years, the size of the deacon council declined because of procedural difficulties and unwillingness on the part of many to serve. As a result, morale within the group declined, and effectiveness in ministry lagged.

In response, the leadership team set out to revitalize the diaconate. In doing so, they set two goals: (1) to lead the church to change its election procedure in ways that would help to increase the size of the deacon council to a number needed to carry out deacon ministry effectively and (2) to revitalize the church's and deacons' understanding of ministry and to renew the deacons' enthusiasm for their ministry as well as their commitment to it. With the church's vision statement as motivation and guide, they reached their stated goals and moved the congregation toward its shared vision. The committee on committees, nominating committee, and deacon nominating committee pursued like courses and knew similar outcomes.

Vision Is Easier to Say Than to Live With

Vision is always in process, never achieved, and requires that we practice the unspectacular virtue: persistence. The journey toward one's shared vision is neither short nor easy. It is more like the Jericho Road—narrow, crooked, steep, surrounded by dangers—than it is like a multilane interstate highway, with controlled access and patrolled by skilled police officers.

This concept of journey may be illustrated with this story about my granddaughter, Jordan. She once took a serious fall in the nursery at the church in Kansas City where she and her family attend. On her first birthday, while her parents were in a workshop, Jordan fell and sustained a sizeable bump on her forehead and a fracture of her collarbone. Later, I told the story to a friend and reported how upset I was by what had occurred and the way it had happened. In response, my friend commented, "You know from experience that those aren't the last bumps and bruises she will experience in church."

We know what my colleague meant. Clearly, he is correct. Jordan and we have much in common. Keepers of vision get their share of "bumps and bruises" in the life of the church. The "visionary" can falter in the roadway of service and pursuit of the vision, but dares not do so. Instead, ministers with vision remember Longfellow's "Ladder of St. Augustine."

> The heights by great men reached and kept
> Were not attained by sudden flight,
> But they while their companions slept,
> Were toiling upward in the night.

So it is with churches. Great churches don't just "happen." Great churches do not blossom overnight. The heavens don't just open and deposit them on the corner of some busy thoroughfare in the middle of some deserving town. Great churches come about because visionaries work diligently and persistently toward that end. They happen because men and women pray for them, work in them, serve through them, and invest their money in them tirelessly, faithfully, unselfishly. They happen because people with vision never give up on the vision and, therefore, pursue it with that unspectacular virtue: persistence.

Visionary leaders embody the vision and support it with observable actions. Much leadership material portrays ministers as "keepers of the vision." Vision theorists and practitioners assign tasks to the ministers: generating the vision, rallying support for it, making adjustments to it, and repeating it frequently until it becomes an integral part of the church's thought and life. In distilled form, the maxim states, "Effective leaders take responsibility for the vision."

Visionary leaders don't talk mission, however; they live it. Leaders stand up for their beliefs. They practice what they preach. They show others by their own example that they live by the values they profess. Consistency between words and actions make visionaries leaders. Someone summarized it thus: "You can only lead others where you yourself are willing to go." Actions of ministers lend credence and credibility to their words—and breathe life into them within the congregation.

Vision requires a wide range of supportive actions. Stories and language, architecture and physical space, symbols, artifacts, and ceremonies can reinforce the vision. By using such means, ministers can transmit the vision subtly and powerfully.

In every organization, people tell stories that help everyone to understand "how things really work," or don't work. Max DePress likens this activity to tribal storytelling that keeps people in touch with their history and values.[23] Stories mined from congregational lore can provide concrete advice and guidelines about who we are, what is important, what we are about, and where we are headed. Likewise, visionaries will choose "illustrative material" for sermons, Bible studies, and training sessions in light of whether they are "vision appropriate."

The trustee of the shared vision pays attention to language. The way we address people, the language we use to describe ourselves and others, the metaphors and analogies we use to describe problems and opportunities—all these can facilitate, frustrate, or foil the achievement of vision.

Architecture is significant because it produces people's first impressions of the organization. Facilities and furnishings can contradict the message spoken and the vision articulated. For this reason, we renovated the sanctuary of First Baptist, Pineville, as a first stratagem in the visionary process. Subsequently, we replaced the massive, thirty-five-year-old pulpit with a smaller, open, contemporary, psychologically human one. Major renovation of education spaces followed as a visual sign of the vision in process.

Ministers in pursuit of a vision will use symbols, artifacts, and ceremonies to communicate vision. When First Baptist adopted its vision statement, we developed a set of symbols: one each for "Where Love Comes to Life," Following Christ,

Bringing Good News, and Caring for Others. These symbols appear regularly in the church newsletter, on the worship guide, in outreach materials, on stationery, and in other ways. They provide ways of "seeing" the vision that we express in our words and demonstrate in our actions. Posters, pictures on walls, objects on desks, and buttons or pins on lapels are more than decorative items. They all serve as visible reminders of some congregational value. Ceremonies, both formal and spontaneous, can also communicate and reinforce the vision.

The vision must be a shared vision, or it will be shortlived. If it is a shared vision, it will produce shared commitment and shared labor and will give energy for the long haul. Vision that comes down from "the mountain" by way of the pulpit will be doomed to disaster. Vision that is "mine" and not "ours" will become "his" or "hers" and will languish. The vision that gives life to a church is one that is permeated with "together." This vision resonates with Paul's declaration that "we are laborers together with God." Ministers and laypersons working together in response to and in partnership with God craft a common vision that they, in turn, pursue together.

A story from Yugoslavia illustrates the only adequate way to pursue vision. Four angels watched God create the universe. One stood in hushed awe as the Creator completed the task and said, "Lord, your creation is beautiful! How did you do it?" That is the perspective of a scientist. The second watched in silent amazement and said, "Lord, your creation is beautiful! Why did you do it?" That is the outlook of a philosopher. The third angel observed in quiet admiration and said, "Lord, your creation is beautiful! Can I have it?" That is the viewpoint of a materialist. Finally, the fourth angel observed in awe and said, "Lord, your creation is beautiful! Can I help?" That is the point of view of God's faithful.

Visionary leaders want people to help in crafting and carrying out the vision. Visionary leaders (1) encourage people, from the beginning, to ask the question, "Can I help?"; (2) help people find meaningful ways to share the vision; and (3) connect them in fulfilling ways with the pursuit and realization of the dream. Visionary leaders know that Peter Senge is correct: "Few, if any, forces in human affairs are as powerful as shared vision."[24]

Conclusion

"Whose vision is it anyhow?" I have asked myself often. God's surely, since it began in God's heart and took human shape in God's Son and was bequeathed to God's church on a Galilean hillside. Mine, surely, in the sense that it has gotten hold of me and energizes my thoughts and actions. Ours, surely, since the believers in this church and I are "fellow laborers with God."

Such vision is powerful. My enrollment in Vision 101 called to mind the account of an incident in the life of Robert Edmund Jones, the leading American drama director of a prior generation. In 1910, shortly after he had graduated from Harvard, he saw for the first time the Irish Players from the Abbey Theater in Dublin. They were just beginning to present the plays of Synge and Yeats to the American public. In one of his books, Jones described the experience. After he had seen them play, he said to himself:

> What are these rare beings? Where did they come from? What music must they have heard? What books must they have read? What emotions must they have felt? They literally enchanted me.

Jones went on to say: "I have often asked myself since that time how it was that actors could make me feel such strange emotions as trouble and wonder." Jones came finally to something that gave him at least a clue to the answer. He found it in an address given by a modern Irish poet to the youth of Ireland. One line caught his eye: "Keep in your souls some images of magnificence." Those Irish players, Jones knew, had in their souls "some images of magnificence," and that was the secret of their power.

Such images—vision, if you please—implanted in the shared life of a church do generate the energy for the journey toward the vision.

Notes

[1] Patti Davis, *Angels Don't Die: My Father's Gift of Faith* (San Francisco: HarperCollins, 1995), excerpted in *Parade Magazine*, 23 April 1995, 5.

[2] George Barna, *Without a Vision, the People Perish* (Glendale CA: Barna Research Group, Ltd., 1991) 13.

[3] Ibid.

[4] James Kounzes and Barry Posner, *The Leadership Challenge* (San Francisco: Jossey-Bass Publishsers, 1991) 83.

[5] Warren Bennis and Bert Nanus. *Leaders: The Strategies for Taking Charge* (New York: Haper & Row, 1985) 87-109.

[6] Stephen Covey, *The 7 Habits of Highly Effective People* (New York: Simon & Schuster, 1989) 65-94.

[7] Max DePree, *Leadership Is an Art* (New York: Dell, 1989).

[8] The American Management Association (135 W. 50th St., New York NY 10020) publishes periodicals, audio-visual resources, and books and conducts workshops that deal with a broad range of leadership and management issues. Membership is open to ministers.

[9] Robert Belasco, *Teaching the Elephant to Dance* (New York: Penguin Group, 1990) 98-126.

[10] Calvin Miller, *The Empowered Leader* (Nashville: Broadman & Holman, 1995) 63.

[11] George Barna, *Marketing the Church* (Colorado Springs CO: NAVPRESS, 1988) 80.

[12] Karl Albrecht, *The Northbound Train* (New York: AMACOM, 1994) 20-21.

[13] Robert D. Dale, *Keeping the Dream Alive* (Nashville: Broadman Press, 1988) 12.

[14] Bennis and Nanus, 89.

[15] Peter Senge, *The Fifth Discipline* (New York: Doubleday, 1990) 206.

[16] Lyle Schaller, *44 Steps off the Plateau* (Nashville: Abingdon, 1993) 61.

[17] George Barna, The Power of Vision (Ventura CA: Regal Books, 1992) 16.

[18] Dale, 11.

[19] James E. Carter, "Dreaming in a Future-Shocked World," *Church Administration 37* (October 1994): 22.

[20]Thomas Howell, *The History of the First Baptist Church, Pineville, Louisiana* (Pineville LA: First Baptist Church, 1985) 36.

[21]David Goetz and Bob Moeller, "Profiles of Vision," *Leadership* 15 (Summer 1994): 36.

[22]Robert Schuller, *Your Church Has a Fantastic Future* (Ventura CA: Regal Books, 1986) 171-243.

[23]Max DePree, 81-92.

[24]Senge, 206.

Sunday's Coming—Again

Martin Thielen

Easter Sunday, 1982, found me pastoring a small church outside of Louisville, Kentucky. In one month I would graduate from Southern Seminary with a master of divinity degree. I began the Easter service by saying, "Good morning and welcome to this special day of worship." After a simple baptism service, we sang Easter hymns, had a prayer, and took up an offering. After a solo, I read my text, preached a sermon, and offered an invitation. The service concluded with a closing prayer.

Easter Sunday, 1995, found me pastoring a small church outside of Nashville, Tennessee. In one month I would complete my first year of Ph.D. studies in worship and preaching at Vanderbilt University. I began the Easter service by saying, "Christ has risen!" The congregation responded, "Christ has risen indeed!" We sang Easter hymns, had a prayer, and read a psalm of praise. After Scripture readings and a solo, I preached a sermon. After the invitation, we celebrated baptism. The baptism included significant congregational response, such as a question-and-answer format of the Apostle's Creed. After the baptism, I invited the congregation to come forward if they wanted to reaffirm their baptism vows. I dipped my thumb into water from the baptistery, made the sign of the cross on their foreheads, and then said, "Remember your baptism and be grateful." More than one half of the congregation participated in this act of rededication. After a time of prayer and the morning offering, the congregation shared in the passing of the peace. We then celebrated Eucharist, using a prayer called "the Great Thanksgiving," which the church has used for almost 2,000 years in preparation for the Lord's Supper. I concluded the service by saying,

> We are sent forth in the power of Christ's resurrection. Alleluia! The grace of the Lord Jesus Christ, and the love of God, and the communion of the Holy Spirit be with you all. Amen.

In many ways, these two churches are similar. Both are small membership churches with limited resources. Both are located in the country. Both are served by student pastors. Both allowed me to serve as their pastor while I furthered my theological education. However, the worship services of these two churches, both in form and impact, are dramatically different. Why? Because I learned a lot about worship between 1982 and 1995.

Although I learned many important things in seminary about the Bible, church history, ethics, and theology, I learned virtually nothing about worship. As a result, I entered my first pastorate woefully unprepared as a worship leader. I've spent the past fifteen years trying to learn something about the worship of God. In this chapter I share a little of what I've discovered. Although I would enjoy exploring such important issues as the priority, theology, and history of worship, this chapter focuses on a subject every minister must deal with every week: the ordering of public worship.

A Biblical-Historical Order of Worship

Let me clearly say at the onset: no *one* right way to worship exists. Through the centuries, the church has worshiped God in many diverse ways. For example, many evangelical churches practice what liturgical scholars call the frontier model of worship. Frontier worship developed during the evangelistic camp meetings of the early 1800s in the American West. Frontier worship orders worship services into three basic parts.

- a time of praise and prayer, with great emphasis on music
- a sermon, usually evangelistic in nature
- a public invitation challenging people to respond to the gospel.

While there is nothing particularly wrong with this order of worship, it differs significantly from the 1,800 years of biblical and historical worship that preceded it.

Early in the life of the church, a basic order of worship emerged. We can call this the biblical-historical pattern of worship. This pattern has endured centuries of Christian history and is followed even today in most Christian communities. Today's worship leaders, regardless of denominational affiliation, should be aware of this biblical and historical pattern of worship.

Early Christian worship emerged from two primary roots: the synagogue worship of ancient Judaism and the Lord's Supper experience of the upper room. The early church fused together what happened in the synagogue—singing, prayer, scripture, sermon—and what happened in the upper room—the Lord's Supper. Therefore, from its earliest days, the church practiced a two-part order of worship:

- the service of the word
- the service of the table

Both of these expressions of worship are found in the New Testament. For example, Acts 2:42 records, "They devoted themselves to the apostles teachings and to the fellowship, to the breaking of bread and to prayer."

This basic pattern of word and table was firmly established by the second century. For example, in his *First Apology,* written around 150 A.D, Justin Martyr described services of word and table as the normative experience of Christian worship. The church soon added two parts to this basic order of worship: a gathering and a dismissal. Therefore, the early church practiced a fourfold pattern of worship:

- the gathering
- the service of the word
- the service of the table
- the dismissal

However, the service of the word clearly had two parts: the word itself—scripture readings and sermon—and a response—affirmation of faith, prayer, and offering. Therefore, in practicality, the basic worship pattern involved five movements:

- gathering
- service of the word
- response
- service of the table
- dismissal

This fivefold order of worship has been the mainstay of Christian worship for most of its history. If we put this biblical-historical pattern of worship together, and translate it into a contemporary worship outline, it would look something like this:

We gather to worship God.
We listen to the word of God.
We respond to the call of God.
We celebrate at the table of God.
We depart to serve God.

Notice five strengths of this fivefold movement of worship.
(1) It is true to biblical and historical foundations of worship.
(2) It provides a holistic and balanced worship experience.
(3) It moves and flows—it has meaningful progression.
(4) It is focused on God.
(5) It is highly participatory; the congregation is actively engaged.

The remainder of this chapter explores these five movements of worship. Although I wish I had learned about this biblical-historical pattern of worship in seminary, I'm glad to know it now. Perhaps it will prove helpful to you as well.

We Gather to Worship God

In the early years of Christian worship, the gathering was quite simple. For example, the worship leader might say, "The Lord be with you." The congregation would respond, "And also with you."

Sunday's Coming—Again

During the fourth through the sixth centuries, the gathering expanded. Worship services often began with a processional. As the service began, the ministers and other worship leaders, dressed in full vestments, processed in. They carried objects such as a cross, candles, incense, and a Bible. The procession evoked an exciting sense of expectation. A greeting followed. For example, on Easter Sunday, the worship leader said, "The Lord is risen!" The congregation responded, "The Lord has risen indeed!" An invocation, often called a collect, followed. Then the congregation engaged in various acts of praise as an acknowledgment of God's glory. For example, by the third century, the church sang the hymn "Gloria in Excelsis" at the beginning of most worship services. One version of this ancient hymn goes like this:

> Glory to God in the highest and peace to his people on earth. We praise thee, we bless thee, we worship thee, we glorify thee. We give thanks to thee for thy great glory. O Lord God heavenly King, God the Father Almighty. O Lord the only begotten Son, Jesus Christ. O Lord, Lamb of God, Son of the Father. Thou that takest away the sins of the world, have mercy upon us. Thou that takest away the sins of the world, receive our prayer. Thou that sittest at the right hand of God the Father, have mercy upon us. For thou art holy; thou only art the Lord, thou only, O Christ, with the Holy Ghost, art most high. In the glory of God the Father.

Today's worship leaders can incorporate these and other acts of worship during the opening movement of worship. For example, a processional is still an exciting way to start worship. If you do not do this regularly, consider doing so at special times of the year. The processional can be instrumental music only, or choral, or better yet—a hymn of praise sung by both choir and congregation. After the ministers and choir have taken their place, either by processing or by a less formal entrance, a simple greeting is still an excellent way to call the congregation to worship. For example, the greeting in the Episcopal Church usually follows a set pattern. After the processional, the minister says, "Blessed be God: Father, Son, and Holy Spirit." The congregation responds, "And blessed be his kingdom, now and forever, Amen." The *United Methodist Book of Worship* suggests the following call to worship. The minister says, "The grace of the Lord Jesus Christ be with you." The congregation responds, "And also with you." The minister then says, "The risen Christ is with us." The congregation concludes, "Praise the Lord!"

Various acts of worship and praise are appropriate during this first movement of worship. Consider the following possibilities: scripture readings (especially from the psalms), responsive readings, hymns, choruses, solos, choral music, instrumental music, drama or multimedia presentations, intentional silence, dance, poetry, or handbells. Some churches sing an extended block of congregational hymns and/or praise choruses during this opening movement of worship. When the church gathers to worship God, any authentic expressions of adoration and praise are appropriate.

One final note—don't give announcements during the gathering or any of the other movements of worship. If announcements must be given, consider doing them immediately before the service begins. That way you can avoid breaking the flow of worship for a commercial interruption.

We Listen to the Word of God

The reading and interpretation of scripture have been central components of Christian worship since the beginning of the church. By the third century, the service of the word included readings from the Law, Prophets, Epistles, book of Acts, and Gospels. Psalms were sung between the readings. Responses to the reading of God's word eventually developed. For example, the reader would say, "A reading from the book of the prophet Isaiah." Then the reader would read the text. Immediately following the reading, the people would say, "The word of God." The congregation responded, "Thanks be to God."

Additional pageantry developed around the reading of the Gospel lesson. When it came time in the service to read the Gospel, worship leaders processed to the center of the congregation. They carried the Bible, along with candles and incense. Then the reader said, "The gospel of our Lord Jesus Christ as recorded in ____." The now-standing congregation responded, "Glory to Thee, O Lord." After the reading, the worship leader raised the Bible over his head and said, "The Gospel of our Lord." The congregation responded by saying, "Praise to Thee, O Christ." This tradition continues today in many liturgical churches. Of course, after the reading of scripture, the sermon is preached. Unfortunately, space does not permit a discussion of preaching in this chapter.

As you plan for the public reading of scripture in worship, consider adding some variety. Although one person reading the text is certainly appropriate, numerous other methods of reading scripture exist. Consider the following options that can add new life to the reading of holy scripture.

(1) Have two or more people divide up the text and read it together. For example, if you are reading the parable of the prodigal son, ask a father and two of his sons to read it. If you are reading the parable of the sower, consider having four different voices read the four different fates of the sower's seed.

(2) Arrange one of the morning scripture readings into a responsive reading format. And remember, even responsive readings can be varied. For example, divide the text into a three-way reading between leader, choir, and congregation. Or, divide the reading between the left and right sides of the sanctuary or between men and women.

(3) Print the passage in your order of worship, and have everyone read it in unison.

(4) Some texts are set to music and can be sung.

(5) If there is dialogue in a text, consider having several people take on the various roles. For example, in the passion narratives, one person can read the lines of Pilate, another person can read the words of Jesus, the choir can shout the words of the

crowd ("Crucify him! Crucify him!"), and a narrator can read all the verses that are not dialogue.

Many churches follow a lectionary of scripture readings each week, from which the sermon is based. Other churches do not follow the lectionary. Regardless of your tradition, the reading and exposition of scripture should be a significant part of every worship service.

We Respond to the Call of God

Worship is not a spectator event. Indeed, the congregation should be the primary actors in the drama of worship. Responding to the various calls of God upon our life is an important part of corporate worship. Many possible responses can be made at this point in the service. Consider the following possibilities: an initial commitment to Christ, baptism or a reaffirmation of baptism vows, confirmation, moving of church membership, anointing of oil for healing and wholeness, passing of the peace, giving of an offering, reciting the Nicene or Apostle's Creed or some other affirmation of faith, and prayers of various kinds.

Space does not permit full exploration of this movement of worship. Therefore, I will limit my discussion to four common responses to God's call that many congregations observe on a regular basis: God's call to faith, God's call to prayer, God's call to stewardship, and God's call to community.

God's Call to Faith

Many congregations extend a public invitation after the sermon. Although a valid method of responding to God, public invitations were not a part of Christian worship until the frontier camp meetings of the early 1800s. Some congregations ask people to make commitments through the use of decision cards and/or counseling centers after the service. If baptism or a renewal of baptism vows is planned, it can be placed here. Next comes an affirmation of faith such as the Apostle's or Nicene Creed. If you are part of a noncreedal tradition, you can still have an affirmation of faith. For example, Baptist churches sometimes read brief segments of *The Baptist Faith and Message* as an affirmation of faith. Or, you can use scriptural affirmations of faith such as 1 Corinthians 15:3-6; Colossians 1:15-20; or 1 Timothy 1:15, 2:5-6, or 3:16. Another possibility is to recite a simple Trinitarian affirmation of faith such as this:

> We believe in God the Father, Creator, Ruler of all things, the source of all goodness, truth, and love. We believe in Jesus Christ the Son, God manifest in the flesh, Redeemer and Lord, and ever-living head of the church. We believe in the Holy Spirit, God ever-present, for guidance, comfort, and strength. We affirm our faith in God and pledge anew to love the Lord our God with all our heart, soul, mind, and strength, and to love our neighbor as ourselves.

God's Call to Prayer

Most congregations engage in various kinds of prayer. Consider the following methods.

(1) One person, often the pastor, can lead in prayer on behalf of the congregation. In smaller churches, the entire congregation can share prayer concerns or celebrations.

(2) Print a prayer in the order of worship for everyone to pray together. Many churches pray the Lord's Prayer weekly or at least monthly.

(3) Lead a guided prayer. In this method of prayer, you invite people to offer prayers of praise, thanksgiving, confession, petition, and surrender. After a brief introduction to each specific form of prayer, allow a time of silence for each person to pray. I sometimes have a "tag team" prayer in my church. Four people are asked (in advance) to come forward and lead the congregation in prayer. The first person offers a prayer of praise, the second a prayer of thanksgiving, the third a prayer of confession, and the fourth a prayer of petition.

(4) Several people can be assigned to pray for specific needs in the congregation, community, or world. This works well as

long as you instruct each person to be brief. Occasionally, you might ask the congregation to pray in small groups throughout the sanctuary. For example, when I was a pastor in Hawaii, Hurricane Iniki hit the Hawaiian Islands. Many people, especially on the island of Kauai, were hurt and homeless. The hurricane hit on Saturday. On Sunday we prayed for this crisis in small groups throughout the congregation. It proved to be a powerful experience of worship. If you choose to do this, however, make sure that people are not forced to pray verbally. Give them complete permission to pray silently. Some folks are terrified to pray aloud, and we must respect them on this matter.

(5) Invite people to come to the altar and kneel for a time of prayer. Many congregations do this weekly as part of the morning prayer. Some churches observe a time of silent meditation and prayer in their worship services that could be called a "discipline of silence." Read Habakkuk 2:20, "The Lord is in his holy temple, let all the earth keep silent before him." Then invite people to observe a moment of silent prayer.

(6) Invite people with special needs (for example, persons struggling with illness or those who have recently lost loved ones) or people engaged in significant life transitions (for example, recently engaged or married, recently retired, new parents) to come forward for prayer. Lay your hands on them and offer a prayer on their behalf. You will probably want to arrange this in advance so you can carefully plan your prayers.

God's Call to Stewardship

The offering is an important part of worship. In Psalm 96:8 we read, "Ascribe to the Lord the glory due his name, bring an offering, and come into his courts!" The offering can be enhanced by brief scripture readings on stewardship, appropriate music, and prayer. Consider printing an offertory prayer in the order of worship for the entire congregation to pray. It could be as simple as, "Dear Lord, we bring our tithes and offerings as an act of love and worship. Dedicate the giver and gift for service in your kingdom, in the name of him who gave his all for us. Amen." Many congregations sing the doxology at the conclusion of the offering.

God's Call to Community

Early in its history, the church incorporated the "passing of the peace" into its experience of worship. The minister said to the congregation, "The peace of God be with you." The congregation responded, "And also with you." At that point the ritual was repeated, along with physical touch, by individual members of the congregation. In small congregations, the peace was passed with everyone. In large churches, the peace was passed to those standing nearby. This beautiful expression of Christian community has solid biblical roots. On several occasions Paul spoke about greeting the saints.

> Greet one another with the kiss of love.
> (1 Pet 5:16)
> Greet all the brethren with a holy kiss.
> (1 Thess 5:26)
> Greet one another with a holy kiss.
> (Rom 16:15-16; 1 Cor 16:20; 2 Cor 13:12)

This greeting, or passing of the peace, serves as a strong symbol of Christian love and community. Since customs of greetings have changed, a handshake today is the same as the "holy kiss" of ancient days. The passing of the peace is usually placed after the offering and before the observance of the Lord's Supper, though it can be placed during the opening movement.

We Celebrate at the Table of God

For 1,500 years, the Lord's Supper was celebrated weekly as the climax of Christian worship. However, the Reformation of the sixteenth century that emphasized word over sacrament, the Enlightenment of the eighteenth century that emphasized mind over mystery, and the camp meeting movement of the nineteenth century that emphasized evangelism over worship seriously diminished the centrality of the Lord's Supper. Happily, a significant eucharistic renewal is occurring in almost all denominations, and the Lord's Supper is once again becoming a vital element of Christian worship. Churches that have historically observed Eucharist once a quarter are moving to monthly observance, and churches that have observed Eucharist monthly are moving toward weekly observance (which I believe should be normative in Christian worship). After several centuries of demise, the Lord's Supper is once again becoming a central act of worship.

Along with the water of baptism and the oil of anointing, the early church used the physical elements of bread and wine to express significant spiritual truth. Through this bread and wine, God's love is made visible, tangible, and concrete. A close study of the New Testament suggests numerous images of the Lord's Supper: thanksgiving (Matt 26:26; Mark 14:22; Luke 22:17), remembrance (1 Cor 11:24; Luke 22:19), fellowship (1 Cor 10:16-17), sacrifice (Matt 26:28; Luke 22:20; 1 Cor 11:25), Christ's presence (Matt 26:26, 28; Mark 14:22; Luke 22:19; 1 Cor 11:24), and a foretaste of the coming kingdom (Luke 22:16; Matt 26:29; Mark 14:25; 1 Cor 11:26).

The early church developed a fourfold pattern for observing Eucharist. This pattern came directly from scripture. A close examination of the accounts of the Lord's Supper reveal this fourfold pattern. Mark 14:22 records, "While they were eating, Jesus took bread, gave thanks and broke it, and gave it to his disciples, saying, 'Take it, this is my body.'" In Luke 24:30 we read, "When he was at the table with them, he took bread, gave thanks, broke it and began to give it to them." The fourfold pattern is obvious in these and other texts—he *took,* he *blessed,* he *broke,* and he *gave.* These four movements soon became the formal liturgy of the table.

Today's worship leaders would do well to follow this ancient pattern of observing the Lord's Supper. First, Jesus took the bread and wine in his hands. In the early church, members actually brought bread and wine for the Lord's Supper as part of their offering. After the service of the word, they brought their gifts of bread and wine to the Lord's Supper table. Today, many churches ask individuals or families to bake bread for the Lord's Supper, and have them bring it to the table as the Supper begins. If the elements are already on the Lord's Supper table, the minister can take them and lift them up for the congregation to see.

Next, Jesus blessed the elements. Early on, the church developed a special prayer for the Lord's Supper called "the Great Thanksgiving." This prayer celebrates God's great acts in history, especially God's redemptive activity in the life, death, and resurrection of Christ. Using the Great Thanksgiving significantly enhances the meaning of the Lord's Supper. Unfortunately, since the Great Thanksgiving is somewhat lengthy, including litanies between the minister and congregation, space does not permit an overview and explanation of the prayer. I strongly encourage you to get a book of worship, such as the *Book of Common Prayer* (Episcopal), the *United Methodist Book of Worship,* or the *Book of Common Worship* (Presbyterian), and learn about this prayer. These books of worship will also explain other important aspects of celebrating Eucharist.

After the blessing, Jesus broke the bread. At the appropriate moment in the Lord's Supper, the minister should hold up a piece of bread and break it. Finally, Jesus gave the bread and wine to his disciples. As you distribute the Lord's Supper to your congregation, consider these suggestions that will add much to the impact of the Lord's Supper.

(1) Use real bread. Pita bread works extremely well.

(2) Invite the congregation to come forward for the Supper. If your congregation is large, set up several stations to accommodate the large number of people. Instruct the people to come forward and consume the Supper and then immediately return to their seats.

(3) Have the congregation sing appropriate celebrative hymns and choruses during the distribution. In order to avoid

awkward handling of hymnbooks during the distribution, print the words in the order of worship.

We Depart to Serve God

After the congregation has gathered to worship, listened to God's word, responded to God's call, and celebrated at God's table, they are ready to depart in God's service. On Sundays when the Lord's Supper is not observed, you can move directly from the time of response to the departure. This is a short movement of worship, yet important. The departure brings closure to the worship service and sends the congregation forth to serve God. Numerous options are appropriate. Some ministers conclude worship with a pastoral blessing such as "May the grace of the Lord Jesus Christ, and the love of God, and the fellowship of the Holy Spirit be with you all." Other churches have a closing prayer or hymn.

Historically, the departure has included several movements. First, a prayer is offered immediately after the Lord's Supper. For example, in the Episcopal Church, one of the closing prayers (several options exist) goes like this:

> Eternal God, heavenly Father, you have graciously accepted us as living members of your Son our Savior Jesus Christ, and you have fed us with spiritual food in the sacrament of his body and blood. Send us now into the world in peace, and grant us strength and courage to love and serve you with gladness and singleness of heart, through Christ our Lord.

The *United Methodist Book of Worship* suggests that the entire congregation pray in unison,

> Eternal God, we give you thanks for this holy mystery in which you have given yourself to us. Grant that we may go into the world in the strength of your Spirit, to give ourselves for others, in the name of Jesus Christ our Lord. Amen.

After the prayer comes the recessional. The congregation usually sings a closing hymn during the recessional. After the recessional the minister may bless the people, and then he or she says something like, "Go in peace to love and serve the Lord." The congregation responds, "Thanks be to God," and the service is over.

Resources for Further Study

For an excellent overview of worship, I recommend James White's book, *Introduction to Christian Worship* (Nashville: Abingdon, 1990), and Robert E. Webber's book, *Worship: Old and New* (Grand Rapids: Zondervan, 1982). You might also want to read Webber's book, *Worship Is a Verb!* (Nashville: Star Song, 1992), and White's book on the sacraments, *Sacraments as God's Self-Giving* (Nashville: Abingdon, 1983). Another excellent resource is *The Complete Library of Christian Worship* (Nashville: Star Song, 1994).

If you would like to explore the Christian calendar, I recommend *The New Handbook of the Christian Year* (Nashville: Abingdon, 1992).

Perhaps the most helpful worship resources are denominational books of worship. Every minister should own a copy of the Episcopal book of worship, *The Book of Common Prayer* (The Church Hymnal Corporation and Seabury Press, 1976), *The United Methodist Book of Worship* (United Methodist Publishing House, 1992), and the Presbyterian worship book, *Book of Common Worship* (Westminster/John Knox, 1993). These books will give you invaluable help in planning significant worship services for your congregation.

Be Prepared
Fights Are Inevitable
Jim Hightower

It was the fall of 1968. I had just turned eighteen years old and begun my freshman year of college. My college often sent young ministers out in teams to supply preach in area churches. One of those churches wanted to call me as its pastor.

This church had called a middle-aged, never-married, male minister. It was actually a progressive act since single ministers had a much harder time finding pastorates. However, some folks in the church began to say he was in a state of sexual confusion or he would be married. (Translation: He must be gay, or he would be married by now.) The church engaged in a heated debated, and the pastor lost his job. They let a middle-aged experienced but unmarried pastor go and hired a young, inexperienced, and equally unmarried preacher boy.

This church called me to become its pastor. I had no clue how to prepare a sermon, so I preached one chapter per week out of Billy Graham's latest book. Every Sunday, people leaving church would say, "Jimmy, you preach just like Billy Graham!" My lack of sermon preparation skill was only exceeded by my lack of conflict management skill. This is where most of us start. During the several years I served as the pastor there, I learned a great deal about conflict.

Some people were angry because something was wrong in their internal world that made it easier to spew their venom on others than to drown in it themselves. At eighteen I could observe the behavior, but I could not interpret what I was observing. I simply knew that some people were very unhappy and that their internal unhappiness had something to do with the firing of the last pastor.

I also observed that some people really disliked other people. This tension was particularly true with one couple in the church who were close friends with the last pastor. It seemed to me that they disliked everyone in the church and that nearly everyone in the church disliked them. They stayed through my tenure in the church, and then they left. I also discovered that there were some real issues that had to be dealt with if this congregation would ever have more than temporary health. These issues were about trust and power, but they were played out on the field of the pastor/deacon relationship.

I completed college, attended seminary, and never heard a word about managing conflict in a church. Rather, I've learned my best lessons about conflict management from actually working in churches.

Not Every Quarrel Is a Fight

I was (and continue to be) amazed at the amount of conflict in churches. Definitions of conflict vary widely, however, so defining what I mean by conflict will be helpful at this point. My simplistic definition of conflict is when two or more entities attempt to occupy the same space. You have seen what happens when two or more cars try to occupy the same space. You have also seen what happens when two church programs compete for the same dollars in a church budget. Collisions can be messy events.

But not all quarrels make a fight. For a conflict to exist, certain conditions must be in place. For example, a conflict can only occur between two or more parties who share the same space or who are engaged in a common activity. No one fights with a total stranger when they have no investment in what they do. Also, we only fight when there are finite resources. Countries fight for finite land; church members fight over finite resources. When prime space has to be assigned to someone, and the youth leaders, senior adult leaders, and music ministry leaders all want the space—beware, a civil war is about to ensue! A finite budget can produce the very same results.

Be Prepared: Fights Are Inevitable

Conflict is most likely to erupt when one party sees itself having incompatible goals with the other party or parties. As one gunslinger says to another gunslinger, "This town ain't big enough for the both of us!" In my mind even this attitude is not enough to constitute conflict. Conflict is about action, not attitude.

If some mediatory intervention is not made at this stage, conflict is almost sure to erupt. Conflict erupts when one party acts in a way designed to defeat the other group. In church work this striking out is seen most often in several different ways. For instance, one side in a conflict actively gathers followers who embrace their point of view. Or one side begins a smear campaign against the other side ("You know, those folks don't really believe the Bible is God's word.") Withholding money is another time-honored way to do battle in churches; often this is added to attendance that is already being withheld. Dismissing a person from a leadership position or simply not renominating the person to the role can be another way conflict in a church is carried out.

As conflict escalates, the other party strikes back. The initial action triggers a reaction, and a struggle for control of limited resources (leadership roles, finances, space, and so on) begins. At this point, I go my own way compared to many who speak or write on issues of conflict management. Conflict does not exist until there is an action and a reaction (that is, a striking out and a striking back). This does not mean that steps toward mediation should not begin before this time. On the contrary, the sooner steps toward mediating a potential conflict are taken, the more probability a peaceful resolution will be reached.

Again, bad feelings toward another or even hostile attitudes do not make a conflict. Conflict is about actions, not attitudes. When someone strikes out and someone else strikes back, conflict is occurring.

Not All Conflict Is Bad

It is very easy to remember the negative effects of conflict. Most of us have stories about the hurt we suffered when someone said something unfair about us as a way of striking out. Most of us can also name the days we have lost productive time because conflict has sapped our energy and creativity. Larger systems (such as churches) can suffer this very same way. Conflict has enormous power to waste valuable commodities such as time, energy, creativity, and even financial resources.

Conflict always diverts us from our primary mission. It is true for individuals, families, churches, and denominations. How can we say to others that Jesus loves them when the world is watching a cat fight in our sanctuaries or denominational meetings? Conflict keeps us from realizing our mission, our primary purpose.

Conflict also damages and sometimes destroys relationships that formerly were health-giving to all parties involved. I, like you, have known people who were very close to each other and trusting of each other until conflict separated them from each other. It is no secret that in many denominations more new church starts have occurred because of conflict than have occurred because of intentional, prayerful planting of new congregations. The negative effects of conflict are so great, it is hard to see the positive outcomes that can be produced through conflict. They are available, however. Let me share with you some I have observed.

Typically, during times of turbulence we do the hard work of discovering again who we are and what we value. Let me illustrate by looking with you at typical family routines.

Families move from day to day going to school and work while they meet their church, financial, and community responsibilities. Then crisis strikes, and all their routines slam to a halt. They discover, for example, that a family member is addicted to a harmful substance. Everyone in the family describes it as a horrible chapter in the family history. But something else can

Be Prepared: Fights Are Inevitable

happen. The family can make the time to struggle with issues of identity. Are we an accusing or a forgiving family? Are we a family that will own up to its failure? How do we want to redefine who we are based on this history? If these issues become the focus of family discussions, what could have been the family's worst hour can be transformed. Obviously, no family wants this type of crisis to occur. Yet, when healthfully dealt with (outside help sought, new family dialogue begun, and old conflicts acknowledged and resolved), the crisis can become the family's finest hour.

Conflict in churches often has the same effect. A pastor arrives and declares himself the ruler of the church. Suddenly the congregation has to grapple with what it really believes about the priesthood of the believer. A church leader has a moral failure, and this congregation has to wrestle with what it believes about restitution and forgiveness. Suddenly the congregation is embroiled in a fight over power. Now it must decide what it truly believes about servant ministry.

Out of a conflict a new, clearer identity of who we are is born. Are we a forgiving, restoring, servant people? Or are we a mean-spirited, unforgiving people who seek power at every opportunity? Either way (or more likely some middle ground of definition), the congregation has a better idea of who it is precisely because the conflict occurred.

Out of this redefining, great power can come. Individuals, families, or churches who know who they are can then move into the world less conflicted and more empowered to live more effectively or enabled to accomplish more good. It is even possible that a new mission will be discovered precisely because of the conflict. A church may know better who its target group could be, or it can be clearer about what unique ministries to offer because it has been through a conflict and survived. These potentially positive outcomes of conflict do not take the pain of conflict away. They do establish the fact that conflict that hurts can also help. This fact is often overlooked because of the pain.

Management Is the Key to Conflict

It has taken me a while to figure out that conflict will always occur in churches. The goal then is not how can one avoid conflict; rather, the goal is to manage conflict in such a way that it works for you rather than against you. This section will deal with what I have learned about managing conflict.

The most important lesson I have learned is that if I only have one way to manage conflict, I am finished before I start. So a variety of options is the key. No doubt the most common method of conflict management is to challenge the person or group being dealt with. In the end, one must lose and the other win. Churches based on a congregational polity are particularly adept at this option of conflict management. In some situations this is the most effective option. Therefore, it should remain one of your options. Although it can be an effective technique, it is a high maintenance choice because cleaning up the mess after using it can be very time-consuming. Also, if it is the only conflict management option you use, you will probably find yourself fired.

On the opposite end of the spectrum of options is surrender. This can be a valuable conflict management option. One of the perks of reaching middle age is the discovery that not everything is worth fighting about. As a pastoral leader, remaining clear about your vision will also help you decide what issues are worth fighting and what issues are not worth fighting. A word of caution is needed here as well. If you find yourself surrendering on every issue, you may want to examine what is going on inside of yourself. Knowing what feelings conflict stirs in you and how you tend to respond will be helpful self-knowledge.

A third option in managing conflict is compromise. I see compromise as a more subtle form of challenge. Compromise, by its very nature says, "I am going to get as much as I can possibly get and give as little as I can possibly give." There is an adversarial quality to the art of compromise. Whether it is politicians compromising on a bill between two houses or labor leaders and

Be Prepared: Fights Are Inevitable

management sitting down to negotiate, there is an element of challenge.

A fourth option to resolving conflict is consensus. I completed my basic theological degree in a Quaker seminary. There I saw an entire seminary community run on the basis of consensus. A consensus form of conflict management is based on relationship. Consensus says the people involved are more important than the issue. To borrow Martin Buber's idea, consensus is an "I-Thou" relationship, while challenge and compromise are "I-It" relationships. Consensus asks the question, "What do you need or want?" Consensus assumes we can find enough of whatever it is we are discussing (power, money, space, and so on) to get what we both need. There may not be as much as we both want. Consensus is the "royal road" to conflict management in a Christian context where who we know is more important than what we know.

There is at least one other conflict management option: withdrawal. I list this last because in my mind it is the most dangerous for those in ministry. I have seen it and its devastating effects time and again. This form of conflict management is the sign that someone has given up. It is most often seen by the minister simply withdrawing. You know these friends of yours because they say, "I'll never trust anyone again. I am going to serve my time out and take my retirement." You also see this in church members who withdraw their emotional and/or physical presence from the church. This option does have its place in conflict management strategy, however. It is wise to know when you or your family have had all you can take and withdrawing is the best option to help you or your family survive. If you find yourself in emotional, physical, or spiritual distress generated from the current conflict, the time may have come to withdraw.

Having a number of options by which to manage conflict situations is the key to surviving turbulent waters well. All five of the above listed options (challenge, surrender, compromise, consensus, and withdrawal) need to be viable options. The more adept you are at using all five as well as developing your own, the more likely you'll be to survive in ministry. I only learned the importance of multiple options from working in the churches.

Let the Last Words Be from Scripture

It is hard to be in church work for long without having to deal with anger—either your own or someone else's. The New Testament has twin injunctions concerning anger.

> Be angry but do not sin; do not let the sun go down on your anger, and do not make room for the devil. (Eph 4:26-27)
>
> You must understand this, my beloved brethren: let everyone be quick to listen, slow to speak, slow to anger; for your anger does not produce God's righteousness. (Jas 1:19-20)

Anger has a detrimental quality. Anger (when I hold it and nurse it) has great power to hurt my health and my witness. Anger of the slow-burning variety is detrimental to me and to the kingdom. No doubt that is why Holy Scripture gives us such clear direction in the book of James. We are to be ready listeners. Taking time to understand the person and/or the situation can often save all concerned great heartache. Hearing people out is the place to begin when conflict situations arise.

Then James instructs us to be "slow to speak." I often do better at speaking after I have time to think through my thoughts and enough time to be clear about how I really do feel. When I am clear about my thoughts and feelings, it is amazing how much better I can be heard by others. I have learned since seminary how much power my words have when spoken as a pastoral person. Because of this power, I have an obligation to be clear before I speak.

James' final injunction is to be "slow to anger." Earlier I have spoken of this gift. Knowing what is important enough to get mad over is a true grace gift. It is striking that neither passage says, "Don't get mad!" Rather, both passages say that when you do get mad, here are some guidelines to help you stay spiritually, emotionally, and physically healthy.

Paul fleshes out the rest of this injunction to be slow to anger. Paul says, "Do not let the sun go down on your anger." James warns us about expressing our anger too quickly. Paul warns us about nursing our anger too long. Paul is not saying that if you get mad at 7:03 P.M., and sundown is at 7:24 P.M., you have twenty-one minutes to control your anger. Rather, he is saying that as soon as you can express your anger in a controlled way, it is healthy to do so. When we as people who work in the churches can manage our personal anger in these ways, we bring honor to God. We help God's people both by our example and by lowering the risk that their lives or the church will be disrupted because of our anger.

Lone Ranger or the Brady Bunch Working as a Team

Hardy Clemons

Team ministry is not popular in churches these days. Team language has been used more widely in recent years, but a church is rare where the people realize that each member is a minister. The staff that operates as an actual team also is rare. Most Christians seem to see themselves as "support for the ministers" rather than as ministers themselves. I will always remember the veteran deacon who prayed at the close of evening worship, "Lord, bless our pastor and his staff as they do thy work this week, and us as we support *him* the best we can."

Many churches today seem irresistibly drawn to a ruler-type leader who sees only himself as "called of God." He tells the congregation what to believe and what to do. He leads from a pedestal and hires (often without lay input) various assistants to carry out "his ministry." In Joel Gregory's words, such men are wed to the "pastor as master"[1] concept. Of a 1991 "summit meeting" in Dallas of some of America's mega-super Southern Baptist pastors, Gregory said, "These pastors were not in the habit of interference from laymen in their churches. They ruled like kings."[2] And, I must admit, the literature in our field says that churches led by such "strong" pastors grow more rapidly. To so many, a team approach seems ineffectively slow and "weak."

Nevertheless, since my seminary days, I have increasingly become convinced that a team approach is a valid option for how the church should envision and configure ourselves as we move into the twenty-first century. I believe we are already at the end of one age of history, not quite at the beginning of the next. Thus, in the words of cultural anthropologist Jean Houston, "We are a people of parenthesis."[3] In our unique parenthesis of *his*-tory, I believe God is calling some churches and some pastors to use an authentic team approach in carrying out the Great Commission and ministering to the actual needs of people in our complex and broken world.

This team approach was not my first concept of how to do God's work in a local church. I grew up in three very small, small-town churches where the pastor was the only staff person. The college and seminary churches I joined had multiple staffs, but were clearly configured in the shape of a pyramid with the pastor at the apex. I never knew, or knew about, a pastor who related to church members and staff as colleagues. Seminary classes did not introduce me to any form of "corporate"[4] ministry. But in later years I began to see that both the Bible and the contemporary church spoke of ministry in ways that had more to do with a team than with pedestals. I saw that church members as well as staff could be led to discover and express their own ministries with a pastor who is a leader and coordinator, but not a ruler or "master." Models such as Harry Emerson Fosdick, chats with other pastors, plus my experience with Baptist Student Union—which was quite team-oriented—led me to take more seriously the Scriptures about partnership or "corporate" forms of ministry.

Let me be quick to admit that I didn't learn everything someone tried to teach me in seminary. My grades were fine, but there were many things I wasn't ready to digest. Experience, insight from lay leaders and pastoral colleagues, deeper study of the Bible and theology, plus staying in regular touch with major teachers, have all taught me a great deal I didn't assimilate in seminary. Now, on the basis of an excellent seminary education and helpful experience working with God's people (who are the heart of the church), I am convinced that doing ministry as a genuine team is a viable model. I am convinced that to "join a church" in the New Testament sense is to become an important member of a team of ministers. I am confident that God is both honored and pleased when all believers find and carry out their own giftedness and ministry.

Lone Ranger or the Brady Bunch: Working as a Team

How Do You Picture Your Ministry?

Upon leaving seminary for my "first real job," I pictured the church as rather breathlessly waiting for me to be "The Leader." I thought my job was to talk, and theirs to listen; my job was to instruct, theirs to follow. I didn't know how much I had to learn, nor did I know from what unlikely sources much of the learning would come. Among the things I have learned is how to visualize and facilitate ministry as a team. "Lone Ranger"- or authoritarian-type ministers may be the heroes of many contemporary churches, but I hear the New Testament calling for service and leadership, not dominance and stardom. In fact, a high percentage of ministry that takes place in any church in any town is done by laypeople—the people of God—ministering to and with each other. Such lay ministry is, of course, more often effective when equipped, encouraged, and facilitated by vocational ministers. But no church can hire enough staff to get all its ministry done. I've learned that the people of God make up the church and actually provide ministry more than the staff or the preacher.

Let me invite you to picture your church's leadership as if it were a singing group.[5] The group you imagine is hopefully composed of salaried and volunteer people. Picture one group with a star vocalist, "backed up" by a group of support singers. Another group sings strictly in unison. Still another group sings the same note, but sounds as though it is composed totally of all tenors, all basses, or all altos. Another has the balance and blend of a quartet, an ensemble, or even a choir. They offer individual competence and unique differences that blend into same-key harmony richer than unison. They offer a unity more profound than uniformity. What picture do you want the leaders in your church to have? Which of these approaches furnishes a more viable model for doing the work of God's kingdom in your situation?

To have productive, active harmony, staff members and lay leaders must learn to merge both strengths and differences just as a body blends its unique parts for viable health. If strengths and differences are to be integrated, they must first be recognized, encouraged, and celebrated. When they are ignored or, worse yet, denigrated, the effective spiritual vitality is lost, and a sterile uniformity results.

In the midst of an ancient world that hallowed a monarchical model for leadership, the New Testament offers a team-oriented alternative. The primary model for ministry in the ancient world was a totem pole or a pyramid. The king was the sovereign; the priest was a powerful, ruling authority. Whoever was leader was "The Chief." Flow charts were drawn from the top down. Work was accomplished by underlings, sometimes called "subordinates," doing whatever their "superiors" required. At the top was a chief or a general, then came officers—colonels, captains, lieutenants—and under them, more underlings who did the bidding of the leaders.

Early in my tenure as a vocational minister I learned that the Bible calls for a different way of viewing and doing the work of God through the church. The classic Christian paradigm for leadership is serving, not dominating others. The classic model for ministry is not a pyramid, but a human body in which the various organs and parts function together interdependently in concert— under the lordship of Jesus the Christ. Both Jesus and Paul offer insights for servant-leadership that are rarely heard today.

Jesus' Vision for Leadership and Ministry

Jesus challenged prevailing views of leadership by teaching his followers what the one clear benchmark of truly effective leadership is: "For even the Son of Man did not come to be served; he came to serve" (Mark 10:42-45 TEV). He affirmed that leadership in his kingdom is not about status, but about function; it is about serving. The focus is not on the power or prominence of one's position; it is not on the "perks" one is granted and the deference one is accorded by underlings and subjects. The focus is rather on the people we are called to serve, and upon the way God values each of these persons. God wants each of us, lay and clergy, to discover and learn to express our own unique form of gifted servant leadership.

Paul's Picture of the Church

The apostle Paul followed Jesus' approach when he described his view of the church and the methods by which its ministry should operate in these simple terms: "We are partners working together for God" (1 Cor 3:9 TEV). We are called to see ourselves as partners, not superiors and subordinates. We are called to work together, more as colleagues than in competition or turf-building. We are called to work for God. God is the boss. We are all subordinate to God. Paul's illustration of the church at work is a human body (1 Cor 12; Rom 12) working together without envy or competition against itself. The church is called to function in bodily harmony under the headship of Christ. Leaders are called to serve God, to serve people, and to be partners.

A No-Staff Team

In my first three full-time ministry positions we had no "staff." At first, there was no secretary, no assistant. Later, part-time staff people did these functions. Now I work with a multiple staff-team of seven pastors and many elected lay leaders and support staff people. I've learned at every place of service how important each of these persons is to the ministry God wants done in that particular place.

In those single-staff ministry jobs, I learned early that there were several people who were just as important to the life and well-being of the church as I was. I came to see our team as composed of the church-elected lay leaders and myself. In the first church I served, this team consisted of the chair of deacons, Sunday School director, Training Union director, church treasurer, WMU president, and me. Both God and the church looked to us for leadership and ministry in that church. If we learned to work together as organs do in our bodies, we were healthy and effective. If we were in conflict with each other, we had disastrous results, just as when the body parts work in competition with each other or are jealous and turf-conscious.

In one sense, we worked for God. In another sense, we worked for the church. In a sense, I worked for them; in another, I was their leader. But there was no sense in which they "worked for me." I was the leader, but I was not the boss. To call me the "ruler of the church" as some now do seems decidedly in conflict with Jesus and Paul. My job was to coordinate and facilitate the work of God through our church. My job as pastor-leader was to communicate with this team and then help them to communicate with each other and the church. This team leadership style built trust and fostered effectiveness for our worship, ministry, programs, and mission efforts. I learned that more ministry occurs and more growth happens among the people when the pastor is seen as sort of a playing coach. I saw that we could get more done when I spent major time and energy coaching as well as "on the playing field." I came to feel that there is no place in biblically-based ministry for the pastor to be a star on a pedestal.

The church belongs to God. God is the owner. So our job is to work *for* God and *with* each other. The principles I came to use in multiple staff ministries grew, in part, out of my experiences working with Billie Hoffman, Dick Cervenka, Red Messer, Judge D. B. Wood, and Beulah Kerr—committed lay leaders. We were the team that led, encouraged, and facilitated ministry at First Baptist, Georgetown, Kentucky, in the early 1960s.

We learned that when one of us did well, all prospered. When one succeeded, all did. We learned that competition in the body produces confusion; while team work produces harmony, trust, growth, and ministry. We learned that there is no place in the body of Christ for jealousy, quarreling, turf-battles, or jockeying for personal position. The aim of this "game" is not to look good or to advance, but to do ministry. The star of ministry is always Jesus the Christ, never one of us human instruments. We are just members of the team.

Lone Ranger or the Brady Bunch: Working as a Team

Arenas for Practicing Team Ministry

Actual team ministry within a local church consists of four arenas: the congregation, elected leaders, church staff, and pastoral staff.

(1) The *congregation* is led to see itself—and then to seek to operate—as a team of ministers. People in congregations do not hire ministers; we are ministers—each of us. We find and then use our God-given gifts at home, work, and church for the glory of God. We may do ministry poorly or well, but when we join a church, we join a group of ministers. To be a Christian is to be a minister.

(2) The *elected leaders* of the church seek to function as a team of ministers. In whatever way they are organized—deacons, teachers, committees, committee chairs, and ad hoc groups seek to be teams that value and foster the good of the whole church and avoid "us-against-them" approaches. There is no room for selfishness.

(3) The *church staff* operates as a team. We have different functions, but we are each important—just as the various body parts are all vital to health and functioning. There is no room for a "them-and-us" attitude anywhere in a team. "They" or "them" is, without a doubt, one of the dirtiest four-letter words in any language from God's point of view. To God, we are all we!

(4) The *pastoral staff* also operates as a team. We see ourselves as colleagues, working together under God, in the service of God, the world, and the church. I see my colleagues as partners under God, not as "my assistants." They are each pastors as much as I am. When a church has several pastors, some basic guidelines about how we operate can help us function as a team.

Guidelines for a Pastoral Staff Team

(1) Each member of the team is seen as a pastor. He or she is called to a specific area of ministry and is the leader of that area. In our church these areas are defined by the personnel committee and senior pastor, then reported to the diaconate and the

congregation. We avoid terms such as "associate" or "assistant" and try to lead the people to recognize that each pastoral team member is called by the church to lead a vital, valid area of ministry. He or she is not an "associate"; each is a pastor.

Each colleague is more knowledgeable in his or her specific area than I am. While I am their supervisor from the point of view of the total ministry of the church, and their senior in terms of age, experience, and functional responsibility, I do not see myself as their "superior." If the question comes up concerning who is "the boss," usually I am; yet, often I defer to my colleague's wisdom. Mainly, who is boss is not what ministry is about anyway. As Paul said, "There is no difference between the one who plants and the one who waters; we are partners working together for God" (1 Cor 3:5-8). Ministry is about function, not status.

(2) Each pastor functions as the leader in a specific area or areas, and is also called to be a vital part of the total ministry of God in the church. At times we say, "Please check with Dr. Wynn on that; missions is his area." On the other hand, we want as little as possible to hear anyone say, "Don't look to me; that's not my area." We don't want to be "Lone Ranger"-type pastors who construct our own little kingdoms within the larger church. We don't want overspecialization that does not really care about the health of the whole body. We want each pastor to partner with the other pastors as our bodily organs collaborate for health, growth, and holistic well-being.

The New Testament tells us to "be happy with those who are happy, and weep with those who weep" (Rom 12:15 TEV). I have noticed that sometimes we staff members reverse this injunction. We are tempted to weep when our partners are happy and rejoice when our partners weep. Such competitiveness and self-serving have no place in team ministry. We are in God's service together as partners.

(3) The pastoral team is coordinated by a senior pastor. The team is not "the pastor's staff"; yet, senior pastors do sit at the desk where the buck stops. I see myself as the integrating factor

of the team with whom I serve. Neither a pastoral team nor a church can function well when presided over by a leaderless committee. The team needs a quarterback; but, as quarterback, I dare not confuse myself with the owner of the franchise. I have the right and the responsibility to give a directive when necessary, but I do not hold most of the stock in most decisions. It's not "my church," nor is it "my team." I am called by God to serve rather than to be served—function, not status!

(4) When there is an irresolvable difference between the pastor in charge of an area and the senior pastor, and such disagreement cannot be resolved by the two pastors in question or by the pastoral team as a whole, it is resolved by the personnel committee in conversation with the pastors in question. We make every effort to function as partners under God whose ministries have equal validity. Each of us is accountable to God, to each other, and to our congregation's system of accountability. We don't pull rank on each other. We have agreed to bring our differences and problems to each other and seek solutions. We have a covenant to talk *with* each other about problems, not *about* each other.

Our Team Covenant

My church staff has a written covenant agreement about how we will operate as partners on this specific team. This seems a good idea whether the team is composed of vocational staff members or the lay arenas of the team. We begin with a blank sheet of paper and consider questions such as these:

- What do I want you to promise me?
- What am I willing to promise you?
- What is your picture concerning how we will work together?
- What agreements do we need to make to be valid partners?
- How will we keep this covenant operative?
- How often do we need to meet to stay in touch?
- How will we revise the covenant from time to time?
- What will we do when one of us violates the covenant?

We have found that a written covenant facilitates communication, engenders trust, and encourages partnership. When we discover that it needs revising, we revise it. Meanwhile, we live by it.

Our Pastoral Staff Team

Our pastoral team at present is composed of seven pastors. We have an operative unity-in-diversity on this team,[6] which has served our church since 1992. We have four men and three women. Six of us are ordained. Five are capable preachers. Each is an excellent teacher. We were trained at three different seminaries. Several have taught in seminaries as visiting professors. We originated in Georgia, North and South Carolina, Texas, and Virginia. We have a total of 139 years experience in ministry, with 47 of them invested at First Baptist, Greenville. Three of us are introverts; four are extraverts. Four tend toward being more practical; three tend toward being more visionary. Our ages range from the thirties to the sixties. All of us are married and have children, although we have had a single colleague.

Practicing Unity-in-Diversity

The servant-leaders in the New Testament are clearly not clones of anyone. As God chose people to minister and lead, unique people with clear individualities emerged. Having unity without uniformity produced what sophisticated agriculture these days calls "hybrid vigor." The church prospered from differing leaders listening to and learning from each other. The church flourished from the blend of its diversity.

The apostle John was studious and introspective. Peter was fiery and impetuous. Martha was a pragmatist, a doer. Mary was an idealist and a relator. Thomas was a questioner, who wanted independent verification. Andrew was an introducer—a P.R. man. Barnabas was an encourager. Lydia was an entrepreneur. Judas betrayed Jesus. They all forsook him in his hour of deepest need. Jesus chose them all and loved them all to the end. He called out their gifts and used them all in ministry. He never expected uniformity; he always honored individuality. He encouraged them and spiritually equipped them to continue "feeding his sheep."

Throughout history God has continued to call diverse, unique servant-leaders to accomplish the work of the Kingdom. Augustine was dynamic and intellectual. Saint Francis was idealistic and relational. Calvin was rigid, an orderly systemetizer. Luther was free-wheeling, a revolutionary. Wesley was a methods man. Joan of Arc was courageous and innovative. Lottie Moon was tenacious. Mother Teresa is actively compassionate. God creates all kinds and calls all kinds for ministry. No clones!

The Key to a Genuine Team

I am not saying that a team approach is the only valid approach to doing the work of God. I am saying that it is far more viable—and much more powerful—than the church has ever allowed it to be. I have found team ministry to encourage personal and professional development as well as Christian discipleship and ministry. Team ministry gives ownership and life to everyone who discovers that he or she is on the team. When we see God as the owner and human beings as stewards, servants, "partners working together for God"—we have found a valid key to what and who God calls the church to be. The proper key will usually open a door.

The key to Jesus' ministry was his choice of self-emptying. Paul reminds us, paraphrased in the words of Eugene Peterson in *The Message,*

> Think of yourselves the way Christ Jesus thought of himself: He had equal status with God, but didn't think so much of himself that he had to cling to the advantages of that status, no matter what. Not at all. When the time came he set aside the privileges of deity and took on the status of a slave, became human! (Phil 2:5-7)

So, Paul asks all Christian ministers to "have the Christ-mind in ourselves."

> Live in harmony. . . . Don't be jealous or proud, but be humble and consider others more important than yourselves. Care about them as much as you care about yourselves and think the same way that Christ Jesus thought. (Phil 2:2-5 CEV)

The key to the apostles' ministry was their commitment to Christ's head-ship. Jesus set the example of service more than stardom. Their devotion to him gave them respect for each other's diversity and uniqueness. Their partnership with him moved them beyond building their own self-oriented little kingdoms into a larger vision of what it means to keep learning to be servant-leaders for the Lord, the church, and the world.

The key to ministry for us is the willingness to live out this awareness: to be chosen by God means to be chosen for responsibility more than for privilege, for serving more than for being served. It *is* a privilege to be one of the leaders in the churches we serve—a privilege to be called by God, and called by our people.

To focus on the privilege side of ministry only misses the point, however. The point is, as with Jesus the Christ in Philippians 2, our self-emptying to God as Lord of life—not the prominence or status of our positions. This key opens our cooperation with each other as team members under God's leadership. Such corporate ministry is lived out in our dedication and self-discipline to being God's servants and each others' partners in the specific church where we serve, and to the world at large. Many want to build team spirit. I find that when we build a team under God with the people, team spirit is the fruit.[7]

Notes

[1] Joel Gregory, *Too Great a Temptation: The Seductive Power of America's Super Church* (Fort Worth TX: The Summit Group, 1995) 319-24.

[2] Ibid., 230.

[3] Hardy Clemons, "A People of the Parenthesis," in Robert Ferguson, *Amid Babel, Speak the Truth* (Macon GA: Smyth & Helwys, 1994) 23-34.

[4] The English word corporate is from the Greek word *corpus,* or body.

[5] See Hardy Clemons, "The Pastoral Staff as Ministry Team," *Review & Expositor* (Winter 1981).

[6] See Hardy Clemons, "Staff Members Shouldn't Be Just Alike," in *Church Administration,* July 1979.

[7] See Hardy Clemons, "How We Build Team Ministry," in *Church Administration,* September 1977.

Finding and Nurturing Volunteers
The Never-Ending Task
Ann Melton

It had begun as a typical Sunday morning. I arrived at church, went to my office to check messages, and dealt with some other administrative matters. I hoped this would be a day free of surprises that staff members sometimes experience at church—hearing from disgruntled saints who just have to share a constructive, but loving, word of criticism so that they might be free to enjoy the blessing of Bible study and worship.

Having detoured around said saints this morning, I greeted people as I moved upstairs to check on the age group for which I was responsible. As I walked down the hall to visit some of the people grouped around the coffee urn, I paused and looked into one of the nearby departments. One of the ladies who saw me asked, "Are you going to be our teacher today?" I nodded my head to indicate I wasn't and told her I would check with the division director to see if he had an answer to the question.

As I walked into the hallway, I saw the division director and inquired as to what he knew about leadership in that group for the day. He was as bewildered as I. No one had contacted him regarding substitutes or let him know that the department director, assistant department director, and both teachers would be absent. Realizing time was growing short before class began, we quickly asked ourselves what was the best way to handle this situation.

It seemed we had three options: (1) Combine this group with another age group located nearby, (2) borrow a teacher from a department that had multiple teachers and let that department regroup for the morning, or (3) have one of us who was unprepared to lead the class in a dialogical study and trust the Holy Spirit for inspiration.

No One Told Me!

Our decision was to follow option one, so two groups were combined. Although this accommodation worked well in the situation, I confess I was left with mixed feelings of frustration and disappointment. I had concern for those members who found themselves leaderless that morning. In no way did we want them to feel they were unimportant because preparation was not made for them. I also had concern for visitors who were there who might wonder how responsible we were in caring for people.

In following up this situation, I found that one leader had communicated with another person by leaving a message on an answering machine. That person was out of town and didn't receive the message until the following week. There seemed to be a sense that someone would be there, although no one knew that specifically. The individuals who came that morning to participate in Bible study expected someone to be there and be prepared for them.

That should not be an unrealistic expectation for those who gather on Sunday morning or any other time for a church-sponsored activity or event. Staff members are paid to be prepared, but they can't do everything! An attitude of servanthood should be characteristic of both paid staff and volunteers in ministry. Yet, regardless of how well you have sought, trained, and nurtured volunteers, sometimes there will be a systems failure.

My ongoing observation for years has been that churches of all sizes share a commonality that is without regard to location, amount of budget, theological persuasion, or other distinctives: A minority number of people do a majority of the work, while a great percentage of church members act as if church were a spectator sport. This type of situation then leaves many churches with committee positions open, Sunday School classes without directors or teachers, choirs without adequate numbers, and so on.

I firmly believe that when there is a need for leadership, there's someone available to fill it. In my years of experience of working in the church, however, I have found that some people choose to ignore the call to servanthood for a variety of reasons.

Finding and Nurturing Volunteers: The Never-Ending Task

Here are some I have heard over and over in response to inquiry for service:

- "I have served my time. It is time for the next generation to be responsible."
- "No one appreciates the work I have done. Why should I continue to try?"
- "I am not worthy to serve. I just don't feel adequate to the task."
- "I don't have time to be a leader. I have too many other commitments."

For all the reasons not to serve, what motivators influence people to volunteer or to accept when asked to take a specific responsibility? Here are some possibilities:

- Many volunteers have a genuine desire to serve when asked. Their motives really are sincere.
- Some volunteers serve simply out of the joy of helping others.
- Others may respond out of a sense of obligation. Someone finally persuaded them to say "yes," even though the match of the task and person did not measure up to be ideal.
- Some people serve because they need the accolades of others. "Look at the good I am doing" helps these individuals to experience a sense of significance and importance.
- Some persons accept roles of leadership because they now have time to serve, perhaps due to change in schedule as a result of retirement, a shift in family commitments, or other factors.
- Then, thankfully, there are those individuals who serve out of a deep sense of call and conviction to serve. They experience the call of God that grasps them and helps them to focus on what God would have them do.

In all the churches I have served as staff or as a lay leader, these are common characteristics I have found that influence people to serve as volunteer leaders. As we look at the tasks within the church that need volunteer leaders, we should ask, "What do we hope to accomplish through this ministry or opportunity?" What do we hope will be the experience of both the leader(s) and the participants? Is this something we continue to do out of habit, or does it meet needs of people?

Staff members who lead teams of volunteer leaders should build not only working relationships with volunteers, but also be aware of personal needs in the lives of those who share on this team. Not everyone has to be your best friend. However, building mutual trust and respect, establishing good communication with each other, enjoying fellowship, and praying for each other will help in building that teamwork. Helping volunteers to feel important is crucial to the development of a teamwork spirit.

One of my most strategic errors in my first church out of seminary was not trying to help people in leadership feel important in their roles. I had "inherited" most of the leaders from a previous staff member, several of whom were personal friends of hers. I was so busy trying to prove myself that I neglected to help them make the adjustments to me and to new directions in ministry. Needless to say, over a period of time, this problem became evident, and we had to talk over conflicts and expectations. Much time and energy could have been saved, and possibly more accomplished, had we established a better beginning.

Sometimes when staff members come to a new situation, they find themselves dealing with some of the matters I have just described. It is extremely important to handle these issues with both wisdom and sensitivity. One of the first actions to take is to talk to each leader, find out about them personally, gain insight into their attitudes about the role in which they are serving, and commit support to them in their task. You may find there are conflicting viewpoints that you share about working with your age group, but seek to establish trust with each other as you begin to build team spirit. I have found that when there are conflicts—and there will be some—praying about them is the first and best action to take. The issues will come to solution, although it may take an extended period of time.

Seeking a level of understanding with each other and seeing the value of variation of gifts for ministry will often alleviate some of the difficulties. There are times, of course, when a direct approach must be utilized. If the area of ministry is suffering due to leadership conflicts, it may be better to discuss other solutions. Often leaders will choose to move to another area of ministry or take a leave of absence. The good of the whole must be considered—not just the needs of a few.

Enlistment of leaders is a crucial factor in helping volunteers develop a willingness to serve, as well as helping them prepare to serve. Sometimes conflicts over methodology and philosophy of ministry come about because people never received adequate preparation for service. Out of frustration, they may hold on to what is secure, rather than being willing to change. Sometimes the "it's working, don't bother it" mindset keeps us from growth and expansion.

Some churches still use the "grab them in the hallway" method of enlistment. This usually means the person is given inadequate information or clarification of tasks. Therefore, when they actually began to serve, they feel as if they are in the dark with no hope of illumination. Sometimes this method is used so the person has little time to resist, and they may be less likely to say "no."

I would like to share some better ways of enlistment. Most of these are not new, but you may receive new insights about how they will work for your church as you read about them. Many of these I have learned, or learned the value of, over the years through working in the churches.

Numerous churches now utilize a spiritual gifts inventory or gifts survey instrument for members to use to discover their spiritual gift or gifts. As Christians, we all have at least one. It is important to encourage people to participate in this kind of information-gathering so that new leaders can be enlisted from these. Also, as is the need of the church, spiritual gifts within the congregation can change, and a person's gifts might vary over periods of time. If these inventories or surveys are used, the results should be kept readily available for reference by the nominating committee, staff, or others who are responsible for leadership enlistment.

Another helpful way of finding leaders and helping them to prepare for service is a potential leader training course. The course may be taught over a period of weeks or several months. Content might include general age-group guidelines, methods for teaching various age groups, basic Christian doctrine, characteristics of leaders, and having the potential leaders hear from persons currently serving in roles throughout the church. This serves to keep the leadership search in continual process so that there can be a "bank" of persons who could fill open positions.

In-service, or short-term service, is another way of helping people discover areas in which they might serve. For instance, enlist a person to serve in a class or department for a month to become familiar with materials, the characteristics of the age group, learning styles, and teaching methods that are best utilized with this specific group. Sometimes people realize they have found a place to serve; others realize this is not for them! It is an excellent way to help fill vacancies on a short-term basis, while at the same time have people test out their gifts.

Leadership enlistment needs to be done on an annual basis. We all know churches that enlist people to serve in a designated area, and they serve there until they die! If I am the person making the decision about this matter, I will choose annual enlistment with no hesitation. Obviously some leaders have more effectiveness in leading than do others, but any leader should be willing to say, "It's time for me to take a sabbatical," or "I would like to work with another age group," or whatever reason is appropriate in order to evaluate the situation. Circumstances can change within a person's life, or the group can take on a new personality, and the leadership needs to change.

Any leader enlisted for a task needs to know the requirements and expectations of the person who is the leader of their team. This is often where difficulties arise with volunteers. No one ever explained the tasks, how to go about accomplishing the tasks, or what the end results should be. Printed task or job descriptions are invaluable and should be discussed with a person at the time of enlistment. No task assignment will be perfect, but there is a need for the greatest possible understanding. None of us want to blindly approach a task. We should especially want to do our best as we are given opportunity to serve through the ministries of the church.

Communication is another key in helping leaders to want to serve, and to continue to serve. Just as is true in other relationships, if communication isn't working, the system—whatever that is—may break down. Being exact about tasks and expectations is important and should require mutual consideration of the team members and the team leader. Usually, the printed word is used to communicate the bulk of needed information to leaders, but one of the best ways to accomplish this is to have a dinner meeting every one or two months to touch base and discuss issues related to organization, personnel, space, church calendar matters and emphases, and other matters deemed necessary for discussion within the group. This approach should be evaluated periodically.

Goal-setting is another helpful way to encourage people to grow and be challenged in their tasks. Goals for personal development, as well as goals for the group represented by volunteer leaders, offer direction and purpose. Many of us often work as if we are aiming toward nothing, and we are pretty good at hitting it! Goal-setting is difficult for some people, but with the right approach it can work. Making goals realistic, measurable, and attainable can serve as catalysts for growth and a sense of purpose. Goals should be set for both short-term and long-term. This helps to set direction for vision for ministry and keeps a spirit of expectation alive. Certainly God can work even if we don't set goals or if we live without a sense of wonder and expectation, but God has planned for long-term purpose. Isn't that a good model for us?

Trust those who serve. Sometimes we are well aware that a group, a committee, or a task force seems to be headed in the wrong direction. Sometimes we just have to let them travel that way and learn from mistakes, if that is indeed the result. Sometimes it's those of us who are the leaders who are headed down the wrong path, so we have to learn to trust each other, and especially the power of the Holy Spirit working in our lives to learn what the Spirit would teach us.

Perhaps some of the greatest observations about volunteer leaders could be said in these words of summary: Always affirm your volunteer leaders. Affirmation speaks volumes to people. All of us need affirmation—a recognition of our worth. Even if you disagree with them on multiple issues, there should be some way for you to find a point of recognition. Love your volunteer leaders. Remember to encourage them with a loving and supportive spirit. They may not have anyone else to value them. Sometimes we get so caught up in what we are doing, we can't take time for valuing people. We are valued by God beyond anything we can understand. We need to extend that value to others on God's behalf and ours.

How do you find all the volunteer leaders you need? These ideas I shared have worked for me, and I have been testing many of them over the past fifteen years or more. The crux of the matter as to why we serve is that God has served us through the giving of His Son, our Savior. It is no small debt of gratitude to be willing to return a portion of ourselves for service. When a task requires a volunteer leader, I believe God provides. The provision will come in God's time, perhaps not ours, but it will come. As Hebrews 13:20-21 tells us,

> Now may the God of peace, who brought back from the dead our Lord Jesus, the great shepherd of the sheep, by the blood of the eternal covenant, make you complete in everything good so that you may do his will, working among us that which is pleasing in his sight, through Jesus Christ, to whom be the glory forever and ever. Amen.

No One Told Me I'd Be Supervising People

Dave Long

Seminary graduation came, and I moved to Alabama, full of ideas on how to revolutionize the church. I thought revolution would come because of the wonderful programs I had developed in my mind. Little did I know that everyone would not be so eager to see those great ideas played out in churches across America. The first lesson I learned was that people, not programs, are what make the church go.

Did all those great ideas go up in smoke? Not exactly, but I did learn that placing people first is where the church finds life and vitality. Somehow I was to do something with these people to bring life and vitality—scary!

As I set about to work, I realized I would be supervising people, and I had not been fully prepared for that. Several questions began to arise for me over the first few months after graduation.

- Can I demand quality work from a minimum wage secretary?
- Can I demand quality from a volunteer worker?
- Can I fire a volunteer worker?
- How can I fire up a volunteer worker?
- Do I have to get bent out of shape to get results?
- How can I "bend the bow" to get a useful instrument for what we need?

A lesson important to learn quickly is found in Proverbs 29:18 (NAS). "Where there is no vision, the people are unrestrained." If we are to supervise people, we must know what we are to supervise them doing. A modern-day proverb says it this way: "Plan your work; work your plan." Set a course for what has to be done, and then set out to accomplish it.

One of the real fallacies in our churches is the belief that "God will lead; just leave everything alone, and God will work it out." God does lead, but God leads with revelation and vision of where God would have us go. So then how do we get that revelation? For most of us, it does not come in midnight stirrings that cause us to leave our beds and pace the floor. It more often comes in the sharing of needs and ideas with one and then two and then larger groups of people. God is still in the revelation business, revealing divine desires to more people than the ordained clergy and paid church staff. Sharing ideas with people is a part of supervision.

The first step in supervising people is to know what you want them to do. Unless you have a map of where you want to go, you will walk in circles with them, and all will become discouraged and frustrated. Most likely, before long you will feel "the call" to another church where you will perpetrate the same insanity upon another group of good people.

If people are to accomplish a plan, they must know the plan. Too often we have been guilty of having a good idea and assuming that everyone would want to adopt that idea just because it sounded so great to us. We cannot supervise people who are pulling against us. The classic illustration of two mules set to plow the field with each pulling in different directions has been the picture we find in many churches. It does not have to be that way.

Bruce Powers has been an inspiration to me in knowing how to help get people working together. With much success, I taught his concepts to religious education students for ten years. In *Christian Leadership,* he lists three "approaches to change":

(1) Power: Leaders know best and make and enforce decisions. The people comply or face the consequences.
(2) Expertise: Experts know best and leaders should rely on them. The people should follow their advice.
(3) Discrepancy: Properly informed people can make intelligent decisions; thus, we must educate and involve people in decision making. Those affected should be involved in making decisions.[1]

The church is full of leaders who use the examples of power and expertise to supervise people. The basic premises are those of leader's authority and expert's authority. We minimize the gifts of decision making we have within the body. This is to overlook some of the best resources we have. A good supervisor will realize that those they supervise are capable of being involved in the whole work process—exploration, decision, execution.

A good supervisor will employ the tool of education. It is not education for education's sake, but education that enables one to explore new ideas, learn new skills, ask pertinent questions, and practice what is being learned.

My wife, Sue, is a music teacher. She uses choir chimes to teach music reading to young people. It is not enough to teach them how to hold the chime nor to count and ring at the appropriate time; they must have opportunity to practice what they have learned. Therefore, we schedule them to ring for worship once a month. She supervises them in their rehearsal and then leads them to practice what they have learned.

A popular phrase in recent years has been "from the pew to the marketplace." That is what the education process should be. We should be working to lead people from the learning center to the place of use of what has been learned. Good supervision techniques will enable the learner to practice what is being learned at various places in the learning process.

The principles of good supervision as evidenced in providing education and practice are parts of the Evangelism Explosion program we use in our church. The training involves sixteen weeks of reading, classroom exercises, on-the-job training, and weekly evaluation. During the process, the trainees have a trainer who goes with them to visit. Initially, the trainer does all the work. The trainees are gradually given small responsibilities until they have learned the whole process. Tested and proven, they are then on their own to establish their own teams and train others. The result is the fulfillment of the Great Commission by properly trained leaders who have been supervised and then become supervisors.

In addition to providing practice, a quality supervisor has checkpoints in their system. Maria Betania de Araujo, a Brazilian, and Sonia Paynter, a Bermudian, are both clinically and theologically trained in the United States. They represent two styles of supervision. When Betania returned to Brazil to set up practice as a counselor, I was surprised to hear her say that she had to have a supervisor. She went on to explain to me that she needed someone to whom she would be accountable for the counseling she would do with her clients. Each week she meets with her supervisor and reviews her cases for direction. On the other hand, Sonia is accountable to the team of counselors in her center. They supervise one another as they review cases.

In the church, each staff member should have a supervisor. One person may be designated with that responsibility. For instance, the pastor supervises the minister of education, the minister of education supervises the minister to youth, and so on. They may function with accountability to one another and supervise one another through weekly staff meetings. The important thing is that there be accountability.

It is possible to demand quality from workers. I probably would not use the word "demand" when speaking with volunteer workers in the church. It is easier to demand something of someone who is receiving pay. However, if the church hostess insists on serving sauerkraut and weenies every Wednesday night, you should demand a change—even if he or she is a volunteer!

This verse in 2 Timothy is a good reminder for volunteers in the church. "Do your best to present yourself to God as one approved, a workman who does not need to be ashamed and who correctly handles the word of truth" (2:15 NIV). "Do your best" implies a high standard of work. The truth is, some people are willing to substitute "best" for "thing" or "whatever" or some other quality that lessens the impact of "best." It is a supervisor's responsibility to first reveal the plan, then train the workers, and then help them to work at optimum capacity. When they are helped, they will be better able to give quality work.

No One Told Me I'd Be Supervising People

A supervisor's work is never finished. The minister of education, or pastor if it is a single staff church, is involved in the selection of Sunday School workers. Then there is training of those workers if they are to be effective. Accountability is also required if they are to be enabled to give their best. The supervisor should know at all times what is happening in any area of their responsibility.

I sometimes hear complaints about Sunday School classes that have decided not to use the study materials. Hearing this, I go to the proper supervisor and ask them if they know what is happening. That gives the supervisor a chance to make a visit to the class. If there is need for correction, it can be made quickly and with a minimum of effort. Supplementary materials, more training, leadership change, or other help can be offered when the supervisor is informed.

A supervisor should learn to attack problems, not people. Imagine what it would have been like had Jesus attacked every sinner who came to him for help. Driving the moneychangers from the temple would have been nothing in comparison! Jesus did not attack people; he attacked problems. If it were a sin problem, he forgave. If it were a physical problem, he healed. A supervisor must learn to identify the problem or else be accused of being on the defensive all the time.

As a seminary administrator, I often heard complaints from students about their teachers and the content of the courses. It would have been so easy to agree with them and join in their defamation of the teacher or the curriculum, but that would not have solved any problems. I initiated department meetings, and we began to evaluate ourselves. We discussed teaching methods, curriculum requirements, course content, and student concerns. We began to write course content as a team of two or more, instead of only one. As a result, we became better equipped to meet student needs and more selective in our curriculum content.

Jeanne da Silva taught with us for a brief time. She had good credentials, but she did not know how to use what she had learned in her course work. She was unwilling to be evaluated and found it difficult to accept correction. She did not meet the standards for the department and had to be bypassed for "ownership" of a particular course that should have been her forte. Eventually, she left the position before we had to take more aggressive action. That saved this supervisor some anguish.

On the other hand, Jane Doe was elected to teach in Sunday School. Her class has dwindled to only one or two and sometimes none. She has been offered training but will not accept it; she is a professional teacher. She does not call her absent members to encourage them. What do we do? The answer should be obvious: remove her from her position. Is that acceptable in the church? It is. Ineffective workers who do not take advantage of training should be relieved of their responsibilities.

A good supervisor should help people to find their place of service in the church. Paul listed spiritual gifts in three references in his writings—Romans 12:6-8; 1 Corinthians 12:8-10, 28-30; and Ephesians 4:11. There are several good resources available to help church members understand and discover their spiritual gifts and how to use them in the church. Often the problem is the proverbial trying to fit a square peg into a round hole. When we enable people to know what they are gifted to do, train them to do it, and then give them opportunity to do it, we have achieved success. Of course, you do not leave them to go it alone; you stay with them as long as needed and then remain available as they may need help. A supervisor's job is not done with the placing of a trained person in a job; it continues as long as that person is doing the job.

Proper supervision requires refresher courses for the supervisor. As a missionary, I used every furlough to study. It was a time to renew myself and to catch up on new ideas, develop concepts, explore possibilities. I used what I had learned during those study times in my teaching at the North Brazil Baptist Theological Seminary, in the churches where I worked, and in leadership training in local churches. Continuing education is essential if we are to retain relevant and productive supervisors.

The supervisor should provide refresher courses for those supervised. If our wells go dry, how much more so the wells of those who volunteer in our churches. A refresher course should not say the same thing over and over, though basic principles can be restated. New ideas, new techniques, new resources—all are a part of being refreshed. One thing necessary for those attending large training conferences is to put into practice what is learned. When a leader is unwilling to do that, he may need to be replaced.

Mary Jones goes to an assembly every year to learn about women's work. The church usually helps to finance her trip. We seldom see any changes in the work of her organization, even when we know there have been changes in the national organization. One problem, which has been permitted to grow over the years, is that Mary "owns" the organization and does whatever she pleases with it. She no longer feels accountable to the church, and older church leaders are afraid to offend her by asking for accountability. Recently I asked to meet with her to discuss some issues that will affect the future of the national organization. She refused. I felt she had to be exposed to the issues, and so I copied a number of articles for her to read. Because she read them, I was able to speak to her about some of the things she would need to "hear" at the conference. As the pastor I have become more informed of the organization's work, changes in the organizational structure and program content, and more involved in asking for specific actions by the local group. I am also attempting to lead the nominating committee to take a leap of faith and select another person to lead the group. Whoever said supervisors have it easy? Supervisors are risk takers.

Supervisors need to learn to encourage their workers. In Bermuda, after someone has preached a sermon or sung a solo, it is often said, "Let's encourage them." That interprets to "Let's applaud them," and the congregation will burst into applause. Sometimes we need to applaud people in public. We can always give them a pat on the back.

I have learned the importance of giving personal appreciation messages to individuals who have done something commendable or just because they need a warm fuzzy. I dabble with watercolors and experiment with crafts. When I served a church in Texas, I painted original miniatures and made notecards to send to people who had done something commendable. Over the years, I have given an assortment of handmade things to people to say thank you. I encourage you to find a personal way to express appreciation to those you supervise. You may choose to make something, purchase something, write a note, give a dinner—but do something to show appreciation.

Robert Dale says the supervisor in the church should play a support role to the volunteers. Structure is essential, but the relationship must be comfortable. The supervisor then becomes a mentor, a guide, a model, and a cheerleader.[2] As such, this person is a hero, pointing the way through the wilderness, an example to follow, and an encourager in the task. With a supervisor like that, all volunteers should succeed. To be that kind of supervisor requires several things.

(1) *Be transparent.* Let your ministry be seen by the people. Do not be afraid to show how you do things. Do not be afraid of questioning a volunteer; a challenge can prove to be a growing experience.

(2) *Get involved.* One of the worst statements a leader can give is, "Don't do as I do; do as I say do." If you want something done right, then work alongside the volunteer. Together you can discover the best way to do the task. Do not assume that everyone is going to read the instructions; help them.

(3) *Evaluate.* Evaluate the volunteer, and let the volunteer evaluate you. Evaluation should be a growing experience. Strengths should be emphasized and praised. Weaknesses should be pointed out and help provided for overcoming them.

Looking back to my seminary, one of the requirements that perhaps did more for me was the supervised field education. I profited from the evaluations and knowing that someone was going to require accountability. Having completed field education, I was asked to be a supervisor for a student who would be working with the youth in the church I was serving. This gave me valuable experience in supervising people. I encourage students to complete field education early and become supervisors where they can be supervised while supervising. You can learn from those who will supervise the supervisors.

I am not perfect at supervising. I am a pilgrim on the journey; I am a learner. I have learned to take the risk to supervise people—even difficult people. I sum up supervision this way:

(1) Know who you are to supervise; communicate with them.
(2) Have clear job descriptions; help each volunteer to understand how their work fits the mission of the church.
(3) Train volunteers for their jobs.
(4) Keep in touch with, encourage, and affirm your volunteers.
(5) Give help when appropriate.
(6) Provide continuing education opportunities.
(7) Attack problems, not people.
(8) Make mistakes into stepping stones to success.

Notes

[1] Bruce P. Power, *Christian Leadership* (Nashville: Broadman, 1979) 38-40.

[2] Robert Dale, "Working with People," *Christian Education Handbook,* Bruce P. Powers, ed. (Nashville: Broadman, 1989) 75-75.